FAST GROWTH

GROWTH

How to Attain It, How to Sustain It

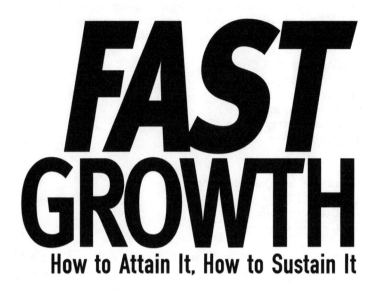

FAST
GROWTH

How to Attain It, How to Sustain It

LAURENCE G. WEINZIMMER, PH.D.

DEARBORN™

TRADE

A **Kaplan Professional** Company

This publication is designed to provide accurate and authoritative information in regard to the subject matter covered. It is sold with the understanding that the publisher is not engaged in rendering legal, accounting, or other professional service. If legal advice or other expert assistance is required, the services of a competent professional person should be sought.

Acquisitions Editor: Mary B. Good
Senior Managing Editor: Jack Kiburz
Project Editor: Trey Thoelcke
Interior Design: Lucy Jenkins
Cover Design: Scott Rattray Design
Typesetting: Elizabeth Pitts

Library of Congress Cataloging-in-Publication Data

Weinzimmer, Laurence G.
   Fast growth : how to attain it, how to sustain it / Laurence G. Weinzimmer.
      p. cm.
   Includes bibliographical references and index.
   ISBN 1-57410-135-8
   1. Corporations—Growth.   2. Strategic planning.
3. Industrial Management.   I. Title.
   HD2746 .W45   2001
   658.02'2—dc21

                                                            00-011059

Dedication

This book is dedicated to my children, Kayla and Zachary. Please don't grow too fast.

C O N T E N T S

ACKNOWLEDGMENTS

I have been blessed to have had the opportunity to work with some of the leading minds in business growth. I have been inspired by many executives and researchers. This book is truly the culmination of my interactions with clients, colleagues, students, and executives over the last decade, and its strength is a reflection of these people.

Numerous individuals have provided ideas for *Fast Growth.* I'd like to give special thanks to the following people for their invaluable insights. Paul Nystrom encouraged me to pursue this area of research in the late 1980s, and his input over the years has added greatly to the book's ideas. Many of my current colleagues have also provided immeasurable assistance, specifically, Fred Fry, Chuck Stoner, Ross Fink, Ed Bond, Dick Hartman, Aaron Buchko, and Bernie Goitein.

Even though literally thousands of executives and former students have supplied me with ideas, several deserve special thanks for their commitment to the project. These dedicated individuals include Lois Boaz, Scott Burton, Ryan Beasley, Mike Readey, Bob Blume, and Mary Opris.

In addition, the staff at Dearborn Trade have given me tremendous support for *Fast Growth*. Robin Nominelli, in particular, was the impetus; it was her creativity and vision that launched the project. Mary Good has also provided outstanding support every step of the way. Her insights and feedback have dramatically improved the book.

I'd also like to thank my family for giving me purpose. They provided support and encouragement throughout the project. In particular, my dad, Leonard I. Weinzimmer (1923–1999) provided extraordinary encouragement in so many ways.

Finally, I'd like to thank God for giving me this opportunity.

PREFACE

I was recently working with the top management team of Caterpillar Inc.'s marketing communication group. These managers were highly motivated, very talented, and anxious to grow their business. To break the ice, I posed a very innocent question: "What is the most important factor that will lead to growth?" "Our markets!" someone exclaimed. "No, our capacity to meet demand," argued another. For the next hour we identified numerous factors that were "the most important," ranging from improving relationships with customers to aggressive leadership. I let the conversation continue for a while and then repeated my original question: "What is the most important factor that will lead to growth?" Silence. Several of the participants looked a little puzzled, then the leader of the group remarked, "Aren't they are all important?" "Yes," I answered, "fast, sustainable growth occurs when a business recognizes that there isn't one single answer. Numerous areas within and outside a business have to become coupled in order to succeed."

These managers at Caterpillar were able to figure out the critical role that balance plays in achieving sustainable growth—something managers at most companies will never know.

It surprises me that what seems like common sense is so rare in business. Numerous books and articles have been written on the topic of growth—business growth is actually the most heavily used performance measure in business. But most of these books focus on only one or maybe two aspects of growth. Rarely have I found an author who hits the nail on the head. Growth—sustainable growth that improves bottom-line profitability and shareholder value—is the outcome of proper *balance* among markets, strategies, organizational capabilities, and leadership—nothing more, nothing less. But sustaining growth is very difficult to achieve. Most companies that attempt to pursue growth will fail. Those that do succeed have relied on a solid foundation, and a solid understanding of growth, its drivers, and its consequences. This book will provide you with a clear plan to think about growth. In the following pages you will find tools and ideas that can be learned and used in any company, regardless of who you are and what market(s) you are in.

Unfortunately, too many companies fall into an "If it's not broken, don't fix it" mentality. Admittedly, this type of attitude worked relatively well in the past, but the rules have changed. What was once acceptable is not good enough anymore. Advancements in information technology and the new economy have raised the bar in terms of the impact of speed on value innovation and growth. Yet most companies continue to follow traditional strategic thinking. Consequently, they don't innovate value, and most will never sustain significant growth.

It's time for a change. Throughout this book I challenge conventional strategic thought. Business models and best practices that worked in the past are replaced with better ways to grow a business. Some of the ensuing advice, such as the "Paradigm Busters" in Chapter 1, will definitely raise a few eyebrows.

Many managers believe the easiest way to grow their businesses is by gaining market share. Ironically, most companies that focus exclusively on market share never realize significant growth. They focus on getting a *bigger piece of the pie*, but for one company to get a bigger piece of the pie, a competitor has to give it up. So unless your industry is growing at a rapid pace, a traditional take on strategy will lead only to incremental growth. Rather than trying to get a bigger piece of the pie, growth champions focus on *expanding the pie*, making it bigger to allow for significant growth opportunities. Rarely does long-term growth result from focusing on competition.

Managers of stagnant companies are adept at advancing reasons and excuses why they can't grow their business. Usually they blame failure on market conditions. In contrast, seldom do I hear a manager of a growth champion complaining that a market is prohibiting growth. Rather than wasting time searching their markets for reasons not to grow, growth champions are constantly identifying new ways to grow their company—regardless of market conditions.

To expand their growth opportunities, successful companies don't aspire to think *like* their customers; many average companies do that. Instead, successful companies develop the ability to think *for* their customers by effectively anticipating future needs. The result: numerous growth opportunities. Growth opportunities are everywhere—growth markets and stagnant markets, manufacturing sectors and service sectors, high-tech industries, and low-tech industries—if you know where to look for them.

With the right mind-set and an effective understanding of where opportunities lurk, any company can develop the ability to identify fast-growth opportunities. And surprisingly, many of these opportunities may be staring you in the face at this very moment, patiently waiting to be noticed. Marcel Post, author of *Travel Around My Room,* once stated, "The voyage of discovery is less in discovering new landscapes than in looking at existing landscapes with new glasses." The right mind-set allows some companies to see things that others don't see.

This book is not a simple recipe book filled with templates to fill out. Books of that nature do more harm than good, simply "giving you a fish rather than teaching you how to fish." Instead, this book explains what you need to think about and the actions you need to initiate in order to attain and sustain fast growth.

By the time you finish reading this book, you will walk away with a deeper understanding of how to grow your business. You will have a knowledge platform necessary to take the risks associated with growing a business. *Fast Growth* provides you with the specific tools you need to develop a balanced action-based plan for successful growth. And the best news of all: the concepts are straightforward and applicable to any business.

1

Should I Stay or Should I Grow

The Growth Imperative

*I*t's 2:00 AM. You are lying in bed, staring at the ceiling, a bead of sweat running down your forehead as you think about the challenges and pressures your business must overcome. Maybe you're faced with technologies evolving at astronomical rates or a changing competitive landscape. Your business has to react at lightning speed—better yet innovate—or you will find yourself following in the footsteps of a competitor poised to jump on these opportunities.

The bar has been raised. Ideas that worked in the past are now obsolete. There is constant pressure to come up with new ways to look at old problems. It seems as though that dreaded phrase "do more with less" has worked its way into almost every business meeting.

Managers at every level in every business are feeling the heat. Companies are running faster races to beat the competition. Maintaining market share and survival aren't good enough anymore. And there is a rallying cry for successful businesses to achieve sustainable growth—what used to be the exception is now the rule. If you want to increase profitability, shareholder value, and longevity, you either grow or die.

*T*wo powerful issues challenge every successful business: how to achieve growth and how to sustain growth.

In a recent study at the University of Minnesota, a group of executives and MBAs identified growth as the single most important indicator of business success.[1] Growth is exciting and fast paced. Aggressive, high-energy businesses thrive and become growth champions. Numerous success stories abound of all types of businesses that literally came from nowhere and transformed themselves into industry leaders. Companies such as Amazon.com, Dell Computer, Starbucks, Netscape, and Wal-Mart are excellent examples. It's not surprising that many executives find growth to be luring and provocative. But growth is also risky, challenging to pursue, and hard to attain without losing balance. So many choose to sit on the sidelines, shying away from opportunities because of deep-seated uncertainties associated with the risks of growth.

Bob Nourse, former CEO of the Bombay Company, had a good take on the relationship between risk and growth when he stated in *Business Quarterly,* "Risk is where opportunities to earn money are. The job in growing a company is to manage risk." He did exactly that. In less than a decade, he grew his specialty furniture business from a single store to over 200 stores. And although there are risks associated with growth, there is arguably more risk associated with stagnation.

So how do they do it? How do seemingly ordinary businesses catapult themselves to the top? Better yet, if a company is fortunate enough to establish a satisfactory level of growth, why does it maintain the momentum of sustainable growth while other companies don't? Well, here it is in less than ten words:

> Growth occurs when preparedness meets opportunity.

All you have to do is identify key growth opportunities and position your business to capitalize on them. It's that simple . . . it's that complex. But how can we recognize these opportunities? What do they look like? Once we identify these opportunities, how do we decide if the benefits outweigh the risks? Moreover, how do we prepare ourselves to exploit them? Do we even want to exploit them? Bottom line, why do some businesses grow and others don't when faced with the same situation? You'll find the answers in the following pages.

Why Any Business Can Grow

Let me assure you that achieving fast growth is attainable for any business, small or large, manufacturing or service, regardless of the dynamics of your industry. And you will be glad to know that successful growth does not play favorites. It is not reserved for only the most brilliant business minds. Any manager, with the right set of tools, can create sustainable, value-driven growth in his or her business. Unfortunately, there is no secret formula—no 100 percent rules for growth (or for any other aspect of business). Fortunately, the answer lies in certain fundamental ideas and approaches that are teachable and have been proven effective time and time again. But that's not enough. Growth for growth's sake can actually create new problems and unforeseen headaches. Fast growth is attractive only when it can be translated into bottom-line profits and value creation.

How can I be so sure? Over a decade ago I decided to dedicate my career to understanding how businesses grow. I have conducted numerous research studies, talked with nearly a thousand executives and consulted with hundreds of companies. Recently, I completed the most comprehensive study of organizational growth to date. These findings and insights have been published in the nation's leading business research journals.[2] I have been able to show, without a doubt, how firms do it. More important, I have used and refined these same principles in industry with numerous consulting clients—some of them household names, such as General Motors, Caterpillar, Pennzoil, Coors Brewing, and Goodyear Tire and Rubber. I have also used these same principles when consulting with numerous midsized and entrepreneurial companies destined to become tomorrow's household names.

I have been getting up in front of audiences for the past several years to share my story with thousands of executives all over the world. Let me be up front: you are not going to find a quick fix to fast growth at the end of this book. What you *will* find however, are techniques, processes, and step-by-step guidelines that can lead your business to fast and sustainable growth. These techniques work—they can promote significant growth in a short period of time. Through some radical insights and some commonsense guidelines, this book will cut through the mysteries associated with pursuing growth to inspire you with the knowledge and confidence you need to proactively pursue growth. After reading this book, you will walk away with action-based tactics, identified accountability, and metrics to measure success.

The book is full of stories and examples that will reinforce what it takes to attain growth and what it takes to sustain growth. However, unlike what you would expect in a typical business book, I don't limit my examples to *Fortune* 500 companies (but do include some growth classics, such as Hewlett-Packard, Disney, Dell Computer, and General Electric). I also include numerous examples of growth-oriented midsized and entrepreneurial businesses. Clearly, entrepreneurial firms can learn from large multinationals just as large multinationals can learn from entrepreneurial firms.

Certain ideas in *Fast Growth* appear to be common sense. As you read some of the advice, you may think to yourself, "Of course, this is obvious. It makes perfect sense!" Let me stress, however, that even though something may appear to be common sense, most businesses don't follow its prescriptions (when working with clients, I cannot overstate the importance of simple, down-to-earth common sense). Then there are some ideas that you may find radical, maybe even controversial. I hope these thoughts will provoke you to challenge your current thoughts regarding how to grow your business.

You must be able to challenge conventional thought in order to grow. Conventional thought leads to mediocrity, the middle of the pack. To grow you have to be willing to break the rules. You can't grow by following in the footsteps of competitors. You have to separate from the crowd. Most business executives tend to drift along with everyone else, reacting to changes in the tide, hoping that maybe things will start coming their way. To help you challenge conventional thought, you will find several themes integrated throughout this book that may make you rethink or challenge what you assumed to be written in stone. I call them *paradigm busters*.

- Don't be market driven
- Forget about core competencies
- Change the way you think about strategy
- Don't focus on growth
- Dump SWOT analysis
- Ordinary businesses *can* achieve extraordinary growth
- Don't fall into the life cycle trap
- You don't need astronomical growth rates to achieve astronomical growth

These paradigm busters clearly call into question a lot of mainstream ideas that many of us accept as givens. As you'll see in the following pages, models like SWOT analysis and life cycles are far from being acceptable rules, at least to growth champions. Taking a closer look at each of these statements will give you a deeper understanding of what it's like to look through the eyes of a successful growth company.

Don't Be Market Driven

That successful companies must be market driven seems to have become the central theme in almost every general business book written over the last five years. However, being market *driven* is not good enough anymore; many average companies are market driven. Successful growth companies are market *drivers*—big difference. Market-driven companies are reactive. In contrast, market drivers are proactive, providing value to customers before customers recognize a deficient need. Market drivers are able to be proactive by effectively anticipating customer needs. Dick Blaudow, CEO of Advanced Technology Services, Inc., a leading-edge industrial manufacturing service company with an average annual growth rate of more than 20 percent, notes: "We need to know where our customers are going, not where they are or where they've been." And here's the good news: To be a market driver doesn't always require a huge R&D budget. Many times, businesses that have developed a reputation as market drivers simply have more common sense and the ability to step back and see the big picture.

Forget about Core Competencies

Many companies overemphasize the importance of core competencies. Ask any top management team what its core competencies are and the team can tell you without blinking an eye. Core competencies tend to force us into a shell, to give us tunnel vision. By emphasizing the concept of core competencies, we tend to think internally, focusing on our products or services to define what it is that we do best. But what is this based on? Usually core competencies are based on the opinions of managers inside the company.

Now contrast this mind-set with growth companies. Growth companies don't focus on themselves; they focus externally on creating and exploiting new opportunities. So rather than focusing on *core* competencies, growth companies focus on *distinctive* competencies—what a company does well compared with the value drivers in its markets.

Change the Way You Think about Strategy

We hear so much in the strategy literature about competition. We are told that you must focus on competition and do what you can to squeeze a couple of percentage points of market share away from competitors. We get caught up in a zero-sum game (for us to win, they have to lose). We tend to imitate, to become ingrained with a me-too attitude. We strive for mediocrity, thinking average is good enough and reacting to competitive circumstances as they come. Successful growth companies' primary emphasis is usually not on competition. Rather, it is on creation, on providing innovative value to current and future customers.

Don't Focus on Growth

Many companies that strive for success focus exclusively on growth. And then, to their dismay, they get what they wished for. Unfortunately, they find out, usually too late, that growth for the sake of growth hurts most companies more than it helps them. In contrast, successful growth companies focus on balance, not solely on growth. Balance between incremental and leap-growth strategies, balance between fast-growth opportunities and operations, and balance between internal growth and external growth leads to sustaining fast, value-driven growth.

Dump SWOT Analysis

Almost every company that goes through a strategic-planning process uses some type of analysis of strengths, weaknesses, opportunities, and threats (SWOT). SWOT analysis is probably one of the most common strategic-planning tools used today. Unfortunately, it has probably done more harm than good. When used correctly, SWOT analysis *can* provide valuable insights into organizations. However, most companies take the SWOT model too literally.

Because the acronym is SWOT, companies logically begin the planning process by identifying sources of strengths and weaknesses from an internally generated perspective. But how can companies identify their strengths and weaknesses if they don't have a good understanding of their markets? Moreover, based on those strengths and weaknesses (probably generated by upper-level management in a half-day retreat), they proceed to identify opportunities and threats on the basis of their current strengths and weaknesses. They literally let their *internal* strengths and weaknesses define their markets. Sound familiar?

Consequently, numerous businesses consider growth opportunities as alternative ways to exploit their strengths while minimizing their weaknesses (the premise of SWOT analysis). Their approach to growth opportunities: "Given that we have a certain combination of strengths and weaknesses, what options are available to us?" They limit themselves by what they currently have, looking only at themselves to pursue new growth opportunities—backward thinking. Value drivers in the market dictate opportunities, and it is the ability of a business to meet these drivers that leads to growth.

Ordinary Businesses Can Achieve Extraordinary Growth

Growth isn't reserved for fast-track companies. Although being in a high-growth industry is great (and I'll show you how to recognize opportunities in these types of industries), businesses that are considered stagnant by most can still create significant growth. Bottom line: Any company in any industry can achieve growth, and this book will show you how.

Don't Fall into the Life Cycle Trap

Why do so many businesses follow a life cycle mentality? Whether it's a product life cycle, a company life cycle, or an industry life cycle, many executives assume that their business will logically progress from birth → growth → maturity → decline. What is the end result of a life cycle? Death. Is that what we want to be striving for? No! There is no rule that says just because a business is mature, it can't grow. Unfortunately, too many managers fall into the life cycle mentality, accepting stagnation as a given. They even go so far as to use current market conditions as a rationale for why they can't grow. Many seemingly mature businesses in mature industries have figured out ways to realize significant growth, and several examples are presented later.

You Don't Need Astronomical Growth Rates to Achieve Astronomical Growth

Every day executives feel pressure to achieve extraordinarily high growth. However, when we consider the simple mathematics of growth, a company doesn't have to grow at 20 to 30 percent per year to reap the benefits that growth can offer. Consider this: A company that grows steadily at a rate of 10 percent per year, compounded, will double in size in roughly eight years.

Reality Check: The Odds Are against You

Before you get too excited about charting an aggressive growth plan, let's slow down and take a look at some facts. Even though growth is a critical concern for almost every manager, attaining and sustaining growth is very difficult to achieve. A recent study conducted by the Corporate Strategy Board identified "unbroken growth" companies—that is, companies with consistent growth in sales and profits for seven years in a row. Of the 3,700 companies in its sample, this study found that only 3.3 percent had consistent top-line growth, bottom-line profits, and shareholder returns. Moreover, only 21 (less than 1 percent) have sustained growth over the last 20 years. On the upside, the 21 companies that were able to sustain growth doubled the return rates of the S&P 500 during the same period—26 percent for the unbroken growth companies versus 13 percent for the S&P companies.

In a similar study conducted by Growth Advisors, Inc., only 35 of the Fortune 1000 companies consistently grew sales and shareholder value by more than 15 percent per year over the last decade. Again in this study, we can see that only about 3.5 percent of all firms achieve significant sustainable growth.

Finally, consider the fate of the "100 Hot Growth Companies" that appeared in *Business Week*'s 1997 rankings. As of 1999, 48 have been stock market losers compared to 36 winners. Although the remaining 16 companies no longer exist, they were the biggest winners because they were acquired by bigger players. So of the 100 hot-growth companies, almost half couldn't maintain and/or manage growth.

That's the bad news. The good news is that over the next nine chapters, you will read about techniques and company examples that show you how to grow top-line sales and bottom-line profits and how to sustain growth over the long haul.

Doing It Right: The New Math for Growth

At this point, you're probably thinking, "Hey, growth sounds great . . . we want to grow, but how do we do it? Where do we start?" Regardless of your business, your market, and the demands of your customers, you *can* grow your business. It is simply a matter of understanding the factors that drive growth and of creating a balanced game plan.

Have you ever noticed that a lot of things come in threes: amigos, musketeers, stooges, blind mice, little pigs, and French hens? Now there is one more to add to the list: catalysts for growth. Because numerous factors can influence business growth, it's no surprise that occasionally we become overwhelmed by the complexities in trying to grow a business. Three basic categories encompass this multitude of factors that can influence business growth. I refer to these as the catalysts for growth:

1. Markets

2. Organizational capabilities

3. Strategies

These catalysts can claim responsibility for growth in virtually every business. And they are of equal importance. For example, being located in a growth market without the capability to manage growth and/or the strategies to exploit growth opportunities will only lead to failure. As seen in Figure 1.1, each of the catalysts has several different dimensions.

FIGURE 1.1   Balanced Framework for Growth

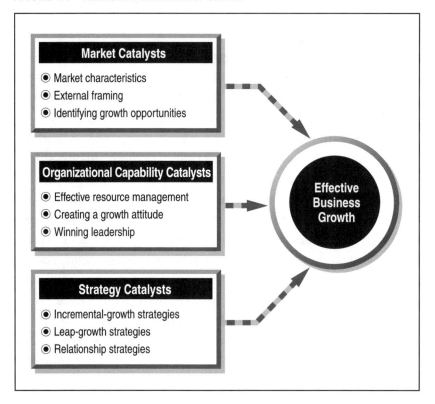

Market Catalysts

Market catalysts focus on three central areas: market characteristics (growth markets versus stagnant markets), external framing (using an outsider's perspective combined with a new breed of insider perspective), and growth opportunities (discontinuities such as new technologies or the exit of a major competitor that create fast-growth situations).

Market characteristics. Clearly the markets that you are in will dictate—to an extent—growth opportunities for your business. If markets are growing faster than you want your business to grow, meeting short-term growth objectives should be very doable. For example, if an industry is growing at 20 percent and you want your business to grow at 15 percent, you can actually lose market share and still maintain your target growth rate.

A great example of a market that has created numerous fast-growth opportunities is Internet software development. In its early years, this market continually grew at three-digit and four-digit rates annually. Consequently, start-up companies involved in providing Internet software experienced significant fast-growth opportunities simply from the market's characteristics. On May 5, 1994, Mosaic Communications Corporation opened its doors in Mountain View, California. Within 48 months and one-half billion dollars later, Mosaic Communications—known today as Netscape—became the fastest-growing software company of all time.[3]

Conversely, if you want to grow a business by 15 percent in a market that is growing at 10 percent, the only way to meet your growth objective is to take market share away from competitors and/or identify new growth opportunities.

Consider Specialty Equipment Companies, manufacturers of restaurant equipment ranging from those big metal soft-serve ice-cream dispensers you see at your favorite ice-cream shop to the hand dryers you've inevitably used in public rest rooms. According to CEO Jeff Rhodenbaugh, markets in the United States were mature, and the company had to find new alternatives to maintain aggressive growth goals. Subsequently, the firm decided to pursue international markets. Result: in 1999, Specialty Equipment was ranked 17th in *Business Week*'s "100 Hot Growth Companies."

External framing. The way a company views its markets can have a dramatic impact on its future growth potential. Growth companies don't limit themselves to remaining inside arbitrary walls erected by classification systems such as standard industrial classification (SIC) codes or the North American industry classification system (NAICS). They expand to new frontiers by looking beyond these imposed artificial constraints.

And having an outside-in perspective isn't good enough anymore. Any company can think like its customers—growth champions think *for* customers by providing total solutions.

Industry experts said the U.S. soft drink industry was stagnant in the mid-1980s. Coca-Cola and PepsiCo had been battling back and forth for market share. PepsiCo viewed the soft drink market from a very traditional perspective—cola sales—and decided to refocus its growth efforts in such areas as snack foods (Frito-Lay) and restaurants (Pizza Hut, Taco Bell, and KFC). The core market had no growth opportunity, right?

At about the same time, Coca-Cola viewed its traditional market in a much different way. Robert Goizueta, former CEO of Coca-Cola, redefined his company's market as "the stomach." This view included all types of nonalcoholic beverages. Armed with this new way of looking at its world, Coca-Cola considered beverages like coffee, juice, and water as competitors. Simply stated, Goizueta's ability to step back and see his industry in a nontraditional way completely changed the strategic direction of the company, creating numerous growth opportunities in a market that experts said was mature. In 1997, PepsiCo spun off its food divisions to refocus on the beverage market as defined by Coca-Cola.

Identifying growth opportunities. As I have already mentioned, managers of fast-growth companies have a different way of looking at the world. They have a different mind-set. They see opportunities that ordinary managers don't see. And they have systems in place that allow them to act quickly to exploit these windows of opportunity. Numerous growth opportunities are staring us in the face every day. Some may never see these opportunities, but others are very astute at recognizing these opportunities and then acting on them.

Although many of us immediately start thinking about exciting high-tech ways to grow our business, others use simple common sense to recognize great growth opportunities. For example, Sam Walton, a small-town merchant who had operated variety stores in Arkansas and Missouri, was convinced that consumers would flock to a discount store with a wide array of merchandise and friendly service. So he entered a mature retail industry with such established giants as Sears Roebuck and K-Mart. But Walton saw an opportunity that the big players didn't see: providing a large discount retail store to midsized and small communities.

Today, Wal-Mart has sales in excess of $137 billion and a growth rate of 17 percent in 1999. Wal-Mart isn't sitting back enjoying its past success. The company continues to push its limits in order to grow. For example, Wal-Mart has aggressive plans for e-commerce. It's experimenting with "Neighborhood Market" stores (smaller 40,000-square-foot food and drug combination stores) and is aggressively expanding overseas (opening 75 to 80 overseas units in 1999). According to *Fortune* magazine in late 1999, Wal-Mart is the seventh most admired company in the world.

Or consider the unforeseen opportunities that Chrysler Corporation created in a mature automobile market. Managers at Chrysler saw an opportunity to fulfill an unmet need for their customers. Baby boomers were hauling their kids around from soccer games to dance classes. Customers needed an automobile with the advantages of a truck and the comfort of a car. This created the birth of the minivan, a growth opportunity that turned a failing company into a multibillion-dollar market segment leader for the last 15 years.

Organizational Capability Catalysts

The three factors identified as organizational capability catalysts are effective resource management (maximizing capabilities to create competitive advantage), creation of a growth attitude (developing a corporate culture for growth), and winning leadership (effectively championing growth initiatives and constructing a capable top management team).

Effective resource management. Not only do successful growth businesses identify opportunities that others don't see, they are also effective at aligning their organizations to absorb the shock that growth may have on their operations. Every system in an organization (e.g., supplier management, operations, distribution, marketing, service) is strained by fast growth. Companies that have sustained growth are well aware of growth's fury. These growth champions can ramp up operations to meet increasing demands placed on each functional unit. And they focus not on core competence but on distinctive competence— how they can manage their resources to create capabilities that meet the demands of their markets.

Creation of a growth attitude. Growth companies commonly encourage risk taking and are accepting of mistakes. They support areas like product development and marketing. They look past current products and markets to provide customers with the best value possible. Hewlett-Packard has established a system called Management by Wandering Around (MBWA) to encourage interaction among employees so as to create innovations. Jack Welch, CEO of General Electric, contends that growth companies "breathe information, love change and are excited about the opportunities that change brings."[4] Growth companies hire the right kind of people to support an attitude for growth. Kandis Malefyt, the director of human resources for Netscape, says that growth companies are effective at finding people with a balance of experience and the need to be aggressive self-starters.

Winning leadership. Leadership is a critical ingredient to a business that enjoys *sustainable* growth. For numerous reasons, any business can create growth, but effective leadership sustains growth. Leaders of growth companies have unique qualities, which, fortunately, can be learned. Leaders of growth companies are excellent at visioning, at stepping back and seeing the big picture. And they are excellent at communicating their ideas. B. C. Lee, founder of Samsung Electronics, was very effective at ensuring that every employee at every level understood that Samsung was aggressively pursuing growth. Because he communicated his vision so well, every employee in the company was thinking growth. Opportunities started popping up all over. Lee's ability to communicate his growth intentions to the entire company helped Samsung maintain double-digit growth annually for almost 30 years.

In sum, leaders of growth companies must play a dual role of entrepreneur and pragmatic realist. And leadership goes far beyond the CEO. Surprisingly, most of the books you find on leadership focus on the leader, namely the CEO, which is a very limited view of leadership. Leadership occurs at every level in an organization. Many times it's the top management team that makes key decisions, not the CEO.

Strategy Catalysts

Strategy catalysts recognize three levels of strategy: incremental-growth strategies (focusing on competition to gain a bigger piece of the pie), leap-growth strategies (focusing on innovations to make the pie bigger), and relationship strategies (joint ventures and acquisitions to implement other growth strategies).

Incremental-growth strategies. Incremental-growth strategies fall within the category I call "traditional" strategic thinking. Companies focus on competitors' products and strategies and many times battle for tenths of percentage points in market share. Incremental-growth strategies are very effective at linking a business to its competitive environment. These strategies are predictable and expose a company to minimal risk, which can keep a business above water for an indefinite period of time. Although these strategies are important, they are only a part of the big picture. Incremental-growth strategies will rarely yield significant growth for a business.

Leap-growth strategies. Leap-growth strategies are radical—they're aggressive strategies that focus on value innovation rather than traditional competition. Akio Morita, founder and former CEO of Sony, states: "If you survey the public for what they think they need, you'll always be behind in this world. You'll never catch up unless you think one to ten years in advance and create a market for the items you think the public will accept at that time." So here's a key attribute that differentiates ordinary companies from growth champions:

> *O*rdinary companies focus on *competing*. Growth companies focus on *creating*.

You don't need an extremely large R&D budget or a brilliant futurist to make your business grow. But it does mean that you must have a solid understanding of your markets, customers' needs, and how you can fulfill those needs.

Leap-growth strategies are more difficult to develop compared with incremental-growth strategies. They seem—and actually are—radical and often elusive to most businesspeople; and more risk is associated with leap-growth strategies. Effective growth companies are able to find a balance between incremental growth and leap growth. Incremental growth often produces the resources and stability for pursuing leap growth.

An excellent example of a company that has achieved solid balance between incremental growth and leap growth is Hewlett-Packard (H-P). The result: over the last five years, H-P has averaged 13.4 percent growth in sales and 11 percent growth in profits.

In terms of balance, H-P's growth has been generated by a strong commitment to research and development in electronics and computer technology. H-P capitalizes on balance by providing a rapid flow of new products and services to markets it already serves and by expanding into new areas that build upon its existing technologies, competencies, and customer interests. In addition, it actively pursues emerging opportunities in related fields.

Carly Fiorina, CEO of H-P, recently said:

> The most important challenge for any organization today is to preserve its traditional strengths while encouraging the creative pursuit of new opportunities. At H-P, we're returning to our roots as the original garage start-up company to renew our energy and our focus.[5]

The central theme here is that to succeed, H-P will continue to develop opportunities in its current markets, but clearly the company will realize significant growth by pursuing new opportunities. Fiorina sums it up by stating that "talk always about preserving the best and reinventing the rest." Bottom line: balance between pursuit of incremental-growth opportunities and leap-growth opportunities can ensure sustainable growth.

Relationship strategies. Once you identify an appropriate mix of incremental-growth and leap-growth strategies, you'll have to decide how to make growth happen. John Chambers, CEO of Cisco Systems, was recently asked in a *Wall Street Journal* interview what he thought a company had to do well to achieve growth. He replied: "Build strong partnerships. Leading companies this decade will focus on internal development, effective acquisitions, and also forming . . . partnerships in a horizontal business model." As Chambers points out, there are three relatively straightforward choices for pursuing incremental growth and leap growth. First, you can implement growth strategies through *internal development.* This means you can basically do everything on your own—invest in research and development to innovate, hire additional employees, invest in operations and distribution systems, and market the new product or service by yourself. Basically, you are responsible for the whole enchilada. Second, you can enter into a *strategic alliance,* such as a joint venture or a licensing agreement, where all parties involved bring some value to the table (e.g., financial resources, intellectual property, access to markets). Finally, you can pursue growth via *acquisitions* by purchasing a company that already exists.

Each of these relationship strategies has distinct advantages and disadvantages. Characteristics of the specific situation you are in dictate which strategy is most appropriate. For example, if market entry timing is critical, internal development would probably take too long. On the other hand, if you have a great product or service but don't have the capabilities to take advantage of its growth potential, partnering with another company may be wise. Although many companies tend to stick with one relationship strategy over time, growth companies are usually very effective at identifying the correct relationship strategy for each unique situation. For example, the management team at Nestlé S.A. aggressively pursues growth and makes a concerted effort to maintain an equilibrium between growth opportunities that are generated via internal development and growth opportunities that are generated via joint ventures and/or acquisitions.

The Growth Aikido

Aikido is the Japanese art that stresses balance between one's mind and soul. It is said that for a person to achieve complete harmony, one must be in balance. This may sound a little tangential, but the idea of *Aikido,* or proper balance, is critical to successful growth. Balance needs to occur both *between* and *within* the three growth catalysts.

Balance between growth catalysts would include the proper balance between growth strategies and capabilities. It is not enough to achieve growth. Growth champions are able to simultaneously pursue (1) growth goals to increase revenues; and (2) operations goals to manage growth. If operations aren't ramped up to manage new growth, a company's cost base may erode, delivery times may suffer, quality will usually slip, and eventually growth can become a manager's worst nightmare.

Balance must also occur within each set of catalysts. As previously discussed, successful growth companies must achieve balance between incremental growth and leap growth. Incremental growth attempts to get a bigger piece of the pie by taking away market share from competitors. Leap growth actually tries to expand the pie by providing nontraditional growth opportunities.

Surprisingly little has been said about balance as a critical consideration in the effective pursuit of growth. Some authors and consultants focus on the combination between markets and strategies, arguing that different market characteristics dictate certain types of strategies. Others profess that the combination of correct strategies and leadership attributes are the key to growth. Numerous individuals have taken their position on the basis of secrets to growth, but quite often they are just spinning their wheels. There is no secret. But there are differences between successful growth companies and ordinary businesses; and to my surprise, many researchers, authors, and managers have overlooked the obvious.

Realistically, if a business wants to grow over a sustainable period, it can't separate markets, strategies, and organizational capabilities. Each set of catalysts has a direct impact on growth *and* each catalyst is tightly interrelated with the other catalysts. Trying to separate them will only discourage growth.

> *F*iguring out a way to simultaneously manage these three catalysts can transform an ordinary company into an extraordinary company.

Until recently, no one had been able to prove a simultaneous effect from each of the catalysts to drive business growth. No one had thought to integrate these diverse perspectives into a meaningful framework. Each individual catalyst may explain growth to an extent but only in a given context. Each of these three catalysts does lead to growth—some of the time. In different contexts, one may work and another may not. I'm not one for clichés, but one that applies here:

> *Y*ou are only as strong as the weakest link in your chain.

How does this cliché relate to sustainable fast growth? A company may achieve short-term growth from any one of the catalysts, but the key to successful long-term growth is to understand the simultaneous impact of the catalysts. Stated differently, the key to fast growth, sustainable growth, value-based growth is balance. Yes, balance, the ability to integrate these different catalysts. If a company can achieve balance among these diverse catalysts, it can sustain long-term growth. Conversely, if a company doesn't achieve balance, it will usually realize only short-term growth. Companies that do not achieve balance are quite often shooting stars; an individual catalyst may drive growth for a while, but eventually the opportunity will fade and the company will too.

The Swinging Pendulum: Lean and Mean versus Fast Growth

Businesses that have been seriously pursuing cost-cutting strategies in areas like inventory management, improved operational efficiencies, and the like are now refocusing resources and efforts on a topic that is so fundamental, so elementary, and so simple: growth. It seems as though corporate America keeps going back and forth between cost-cutting strategies (a.k.a. downsizing, outsourcing, reengineering) and growth so that we create chaos, not balance. These concepts are so basic that it's amazing leaders of organizations pursue one and completely forget about the other.

So, why is growth so hot? What's in it for you and for your company? Figure 1.2 shows you six good reasons to grow your business.

A direct link between growth and value. Fast-growth companies are perceived as attractive and are rewarded with high profit-to-earnings ratios.[6] In contrast, slower growing companies are perceived as boring, behind the times, and out of touch; and they are valued accordingly. Therefore, managers feel a tremendous pressure to grow their businesses. Today's investors put a much higher value on companies that improve their bottom-line profits through sales growth rather than through cost cutting.[7]

A recent study performed by Mercer Management Consulting showed that fast-growth companies consistently outperformed slow-growth companies. Specifically, over a five-year period, growth companies yielded a 19 percent average annual return to shareholders, whereas slow-growth companies averaged an annual return of only about 5 percent. Companies that generate profits from growing revenues are much better prepared to sustain profits over a long period compared with com-

FIGURE 1.2   Benefits of Growth

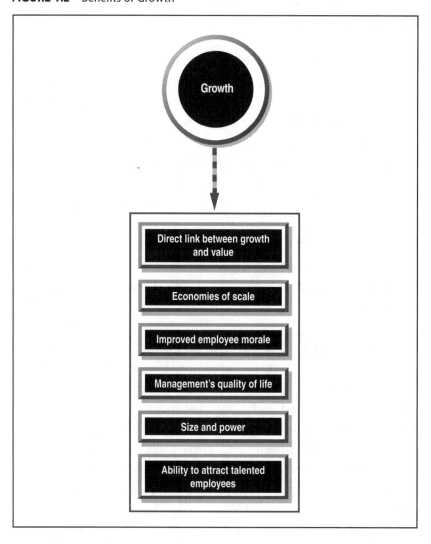

panies that generate profit as a result of cost cutting. It's common to see statements of leading organizations professing that continuous growth in sales and profits are basic necessities to create shareholder value and achieve other objectives. Chuck Knight, former CEO of Emerson Electric, knows the value of growth (versus cost cutting) to drive long-term value. He turned Emerson Electric from a cost-cutting machine into a growth champion. He notes: "We got so bottom-line oriented that we were inhibiting growth. We were cutting, cutting. But you can only go so far."

Economies of scale. Growth is simply an increase in organizational size. The larger a business becomes, the more economies of scale it will realize. Economies of scale lead to cost savings in numerous ways, ranging from the efficiencies gained by larger production facilities to the ability to buy larger quantities of raw materials. We can clearly see the impact of improved economies of scale in industries such as pharmaceuticals and telecommunications.

Improved employee morale. We all want to be on the winning team. It's more rewarding to work for a growth company than for a stagnant company. Stated simply, working for fast-growth companies is more fun. During a recent conversation with employees of a fast-growth division at Caterpillar, the division manager told me that her employees look forward to coming into work everyday because of the exciting opportunities to grow their business. Bottom line: the employees in this group show considerable pride in their work. They assume ownership.

Growth also provides employees with a broader range of promotional opportunities. As a business grows, new layers are inevitably created, and, consequently, new managers are needed. This creates opportunities for personal growth and increased rewards. Not only is this a bonus for current employees, but it entices talented recruits to work for fast-growth companies.

Management's quality of life. Would you rather go into a shareholder meeting to make a presentation that illustrates how you cut costs last quarter or to make a presentation about how you were able to grow revenues last quarter? Managers of growth companies have less conflict with shareholders, with the board of directors, and with employees.

Size and power. Larger businesses have more power than smaller businesses. Larger businesses can take a hit on the chin and come back tomorrow to start all over, whereas smaller businesses may be knocked out. As Jack Welch states, "Size gives us another big advantage; our reach and resources enable us to go to bat more frequently, to take more swings, to experiment more, and unlike a small company, we can miss on occasion and get to swing again."[8]

Ability to attract talented employees. Growth companies attract top-caliber employees. The best of the best are attracted to companies that challenge them and provide the best opportunity for advancement. Hewlett-Packard's position: "Growth is also important in order to attract and retain high-caliber people. These individuals will align their future only with a company that offers them considerable opportunity for personal progress. Opportunities are greater and more challenging in a growing company."[9]

The environment in growth companies is alive. Wouldn't you rather work in a company that focuses on possibilities rather than on constraints?

Letting the Pendulum Swing Too Far: When Good Growth Becomes Bad

Be careful. Bigger is not always better. There is a huge difference between growing to live and living to grow. The latter, growing for the sake of growth, can actually destroy a company. Companies caught in the trap of growing at all costs tend to lose sight of the ultimate goal of their company: sustainable value creation. Growth for the sake of growth may lead to overambitious investments that deplete a business of its critical resources or to invest in an acquisition that will never yield a positive return.

Desperation for growth may lead to risky diversification into uncharted waters. Although sales may increase, the company has no reason to be in these markets. Sales may increase, but profitability and ultimately value are hurt. For example, German-based auto manufacturer Daimler-Benz has shown that a company can grow bigger in terms of sales revenues without enhancing profitability and value to shareholders.

If a company grows too fast, it may lose its sources of competitive advantage. Numerous stories of companies that grew too fast for their own good abound. Orders keep coming in faster than the company can supply. Then orders fall behind, quality starts to slip, and the company loses efficiencies in everything from customer service to accounts receivable.

Floyd Feezell, an entrepreneurial engineer, experienced numerous problems from growing too big too fast.[10] An engineering company he joined in 1985 grew at an average rate of over 50 percent for six years in a row. "We saw the many stresses and strains of rapid growth." New employees were brought in and put on the front line before they were ready, the company lost all sense of continuity, and ultimately customers became frustrated. Growth eventually took its toll. Feezell recalls that "internal stresses developed and the company essentially split in half." Eventually, Feezell had to spin off a new company, SCA Engineering. He has learned the hard way of the many hidden dangers associated with growth, especially fast growth.

Don't let the downside of growth discourage your desire to grow. Most of the downside can be virtually eliminated through a well-balanced business plan, as presented in this book.

Ready, Set, Grow: A Unique Approach to Growth

We don't learn just from the companies that have grown successfully; we also learn from companies that have tried to grow but failed. By limiting research and examples exclusively to growth companies, we're putting on blinders, ignoring many of the downside risks associated with growth—we're only getting half the story. Rather than finding case studies of the most successful growth companies and then trying to figure out how to imitate them, the methods and techniques in this book are based on research that explains why certain companies grow and why others don't. The ideas here represent the most comprehensive, in-depth discussion of growth. Discussions of markets, capabilities, and strategies are not new, but the integrative approaches and collection of practical guidelines are unique.

In sum, the three major catalysts for growth are markets, capabilities, and strategies; and a section is devoted to each of these catalysts. The topics identified in Figure 1.1 provide the outline for the next three sections of the book. The final section brings everything together in a comprehensive, integrative framework to provide your business with a balanced plan of attack to achieve fast and sustainable growth.

Growth doesn't just happen. It takes a lot of planning and a lot of work. A business must nurture growth as a farmer nurtures his crops. Imagine that you're given a plot of land. The land has substantial potential, but if you just sit there and stare at it, nothing will happen. To cultivate your crops, you must first plant your seeds, then ensure that the land receives the proper nutrients and water. By carefully planning how to best use his plot of land and then tending to its needs, a farmer receives his just rewards. In business, growth takes a lot of planning. You must carefully plan and then take the necessary actions to ensure that your business receives the proper nutrients to realize growth.

It doesn't matter what kind of business you are in (large versus small, public versus private, manufacturing versus service, profit versus not-for-profit). These guidelines have been carefully developed by studying hundreds of companies and have then been tested in the ultimate laboratory: industry. Every idea presented in this book is a proven technique that has worked time and again to help some companies attain astronomical growth rates.

Remember, all you have to do is identify opportunities and capitalize on them. There may be no easy answers, but there are qualities found in fast-growth companies that aren't found in more stagnant organizations. The following pages provide you with effective techniques to identify growth opportunities, commonsense guidelines to position your business to respond quickly to these growth opportunities, and winning strategies to create a balanced plan of attack.

Endnotes

1. Gary Hubbard and Philip Bromiley, "What Organizational Theories Say about How Firms Measure Performance" (paper presented at the Strategic Management Society Meetings, Mexico City, Mexico, October 1995).

2. I have published over 40 articles on organizational growth that have appeared in numerous research-based journals. A sample includes: Laurence G. Weinzimmer, "A Replication and Extension of Organizational Growth Determinants," *Journal of Business Research* 48, no. 1 (2000): 35–42; Laurence G. Weinzimmer, Paul C. Nystrom, and Sarah J. Freeman, "Methods for Measuring Organizational Growth: Issues, Consequences, and Contingencies," *Journal of Management* 24, no. 2 (1998): 235–62; Laurence G. Weinzimmer, "Top Management Team Determinants of Organizational Growth in a Small Business Context: A Comparative Study," *Journal of Small Business Management* 35, no. 3 (1997): 1–10; Laurence G. Weinzimmer, Fred L. Fry, and Paul C. Nystrom, "The Search for Opportunities by Small Business Owners," *Journal of Small Business Strategy* 7, no. 3 (1996): 1–14; Laurence G. Weinzimmer, Robert Robinson, and Ross L. Fink, "Small Business Entry Strategies: An Integration of Technological Discontinuity and Industry Growth Potential, *Journal of Small Business Strategy* 5, no. 1 (1994): 1–10.

3. David B. Yoffie and Michael A. Cusumano, "Building a Company on Internet Time: Lessons from Netscape," *California Management Review* 41, no. 3 (Spring 1999): 8–28.

4. Jack Welch, "Growth Initiatives," *Executive Excellence* 16, no. 6 (June 1999): 8–9.

5. Year 2000 Outlook Conference, San Francisco, 14 January 2000.

6. Laurence G. Weinzimmer, "The Impact of Organizational Growth on Financial Performance," working paper, 2000.

7. Edward W. Barnholt, "Fostering Business Growth with Breakthrough Innovation," *Research Technology Management* (March-April 1997): 12–16.

8. Welch, "Growth Initiatives."

9. <www.H-P.com>.

10. Laurie A. Shuster, "Growing Pains," *Civil Engineering* (May 1999): 64–65.

ONE

Market Catalysts
Understanding, Identifying, and Creating Fast-Growth Opportunities

*I*f you are like most executives, the majority of your energies are focused on putting out fires. Whenever you get a refreshing breath of the big picture, it's quickly choked off by short-term competitive pressures.

Why is it that most companies cannot figure out how to grow their businesses when countless opportunities are right under their noses? It's a matter of framing, a different way of looking at the world. Growth champions have an uncanny ability to develop in-depth knowledge of their markets and supercharge that knowledge with leading-edge expertise in their business. This allows them to anticipate where their markets are going better than anyone else.

In the next two chapters, you'll see how growth champions look at markets in different ways than most companies do and learn how they see more opportunities. The broader your scope, the more opportunities you will come across. There is no such thing as a lucky firm. All of us are faced with opportunities every day—some choose to see them, others choose to look the other way. This section not only tells you *how* to look but it justifies *why* you should look, and, most important, it tells you *where* to look.

2

External Framing

Conquering New Frontiers

I find it ironic that so many average managers take credit when their companies do well but blame market factors when their companies experience a downturn. "Our markets are slumping, and we won't be able to grow until they turn around," they say. Or maybe, "Competition is so fierce that there's just not enough market share to go around for everyone and that's why we can't grow." They can come up with some very creative excuses to explain why they can't grow their businesses.

In contrast, seldom do I hear a manager of a growth champion complaining that a market is prohibiting growth. Rather than wasting time searching their markets for reasons not to grow, growth champions are constantly identifying new ways to grow their companies—regardless of market conditions. Arguably, it's easier to succeed in a growth market compared to a stagnant market. But there are numerous examples of companies that continue to grow in mature markets. Companies like Starbucks, Wal-Mart, and Disney are clearly growth champions;

and all achieved this status in what most would view as mature, low-growth markets.

> *T*he difference between stagnant companies and growth champions is as simple as how they perceive their respective markets.

To position your company to break away from the crowd and rise to the top, it's important to understand how growth champions view markets—to think like a growth champion. Most companies can't figure out how to grow their businesses because they view their markets in traditional ways, often focusing on their competition. Growth champions, on the other hand, view their markets in distinctly different ways by focusing on value innovation.

It's not surprising that given the same situation, an average company may see a hopeless, disparate environment, whereas a growth champion sees a market filled with an abundance of opportunities. One reason for this difference is that most companies focus on the past and present rather than harnessing their efforts to focus on the future. Unfortunately, these companies bury themselves in historical data to try to get a grip on what's happening today. Admittedly, growth companies *use* historical data too, but they *focus* their efforts on tomorrow rather than today, effectively anticipating future needs. Variations in how companies understand and view their markets can be summed up as follows:

> *A*verage companies are reactive to changes; they are driven by markets.
>   Growth companies proactively anticipate change; they drive markets.

The National Hockey League's (NHL's) Wayne Gretsky used the same principle that growth companies use to become one of the greatest hockey players of all time. In what has become one of the more heavily cited interviews in recent years, Gretsky was asked why he is so much better than other players. Rather than saying he is a faster skater or a physically dominating player, Gretsky simply stated that most players skate to where the puck already is, but he skates to where the puck will be. Gretsky attributes his success to his ability to anticipate, which he did better than anyone else who ever played the game. This same characteristic is true of most successful companies— they are able to anticipate where their markets are going better than any other company in the same markets. How do growth companies do it? How can they see things that others cannot? It's not a matter of some elaborate analytic system or the ability to look into a crystal ball. Growth companies can anticipate markets because they have a solid understanding of what it takes to innovate value. The better you understand value innovation, the more opportunities you'll discover for your business.

Value Innovation: Being a Market Driver versus Being Market Driven

If a company wants to position itself for significant, sustainable growth, it must first embrace the concept of value innovation. Growth champions drive markets proactively as opposed to being market driven. Although a lot of companies talk about *value creation,* only a select few talk about *value innovation.* Value creation and value innovation are not the same. Value creation is usually an incremental improvement over existing products or services, usually in reaction to customer demand. Many times value creation is used as a metric to convince customers they should pay more. In contrast, value innovators think proactively in terms of providing total solutions for customers' needs—often before customers realize a need exists. (Value innovation is discussed in more detail in Chapter 6 when I introduce alternative growth strategies.)

I learned about the power of value innovation at a very young age. I grew up in the northern suburbs of Chicago, and every summer while I was a kid, I would drag a rusty old lawn mower behind me, going door-to-door to ask my neighbors if I could cut their lawn. If you had asked me what I was doing, I would have probably given you a strange look and replied, "I'm cutting grass." Then it hit me one day that I wasn't just cutting grass, I was improving the physical appearance of my customers' houses. What else could I do to improve the physical appearance of my customers' homes? How could I become a one-stop shop for all of my customers' home beautification needs? I started informing neighbors that I could do other gardening jobs. I began planting flowers and shrubs, and more business rolled in. I had to enlist my brother and a few friends to keep up with the demand.

By the time I was in high school, I had expanded into painting houses. Then, during the summers of my college years, a friend and I had our own home improvement business, providing total solutions for our customers' needs. We designed and built multilevel decks, installed brick and flagstone patios, built fountains, laid sod, and put in trees and fencing (in addition to cutting lawns, of course). Here I was, a college student, and I was pulling in a five-figure income during a few months off in the summer while earning my undergraduate degree. There were, of course, other kids in other neighborhoods that also cut grass during the summer—that's all they did. Understanding the needs of your customers and then delivering value will create significant opportunities for growth.

Changing Focus

The idea of value innovation challenges conventional strategic management ideas. Conventional strategy suggests that companies should focus their energies on beating the competition. We tend to play follow the leader, focusing on competition rather than customers. Companies that adhere to traditional strategies are likely to end up losers in the long run. Those that effectively focus on value innovation are poised to move to the top. W. Chan Kim and Renee Mauborgne, experts on value innovation, contend that "competition provides a sticky starting point for strategic thinking. A focus on matching and beating competition leads to reactive, incremental, and often imitative strategic moves."[1]

This is not to say that successful growth companies ignore competition; that could prove very foolish. However, their focal point is on customer value rather than on keeping up with the Joneses. I often hear from managers at companies that have changed their focal point from competition to customer value. Most of them agree that when they focused on competition, they were able to keep pace with the competitive market. However, effectively focusing on customer value keeps them *ahead* of the competitive market.

Competition should not be ignored, but it should not be the focal point for growth.

Consider IBM and Compaq in the mid-1980s PC market. When Compaq introduced its IBM-compatible computers with improved quality at a cost 10 to 15 percent lower than the IBM machines, it quickly won market share. IBM responded by trying to develop features more sophisticated than Compaq's. This triggered Compaq to focus on beating IBM. By focusing on trying to surpass each other in the race to gain market share, both companies' machines became overly sophisticated and overly priced. Both companies were so busy trying to beat each other that neither realized customers were more concerned about user friendliness and price. IBM and Compaq were both so concerned with each other that they never anticipated the low-end computer market. As IBM began to go downhill in the late 1980s, Compaq was marching right behind. Companies that were able to effectively understand customer value—companies like Dell and Gateway—figured out better ways to meet customer needs. And it was not until 1991 that Compaq finally stopped focusing on competition and started focusing on value, transforming itself from a market share loser (like IBM) into the top player in the market.

Compare the competitive-oriented tactics of IBM and Compaq with the value-oriented approach used by the Calloway Golf Company. Calloway is a U.S.-based manufacturer of golf clubs that has quickly risen to the top of its industry. Calloway has never focused on competition. Other manufacturers, such as Wilson, Kartsen, and Dunlop, focused on cost and designing clubs that would carry golf balls farther; their clubs looked alike as a result of competitive benchmarking. Then, along came Calloway. Unlike its competitors, Calloway focused on why the majority of people played golf in the first place—it was to have fun. While competitive golfers wanted features offered by other manufacturers' golf clubs, most weekend golfers just wanted to enjoy themselves. What better way to have fun than make the game easier. Calloway designed golf clubs with larger heads, a design that made it easier to hit the ball. Calloway's ability to understand customers' needs gave it the largest share of the overall market. Eventually, Calloway also became overwhelmingly popular with PGA players, and its club designs have even been credited with drawing new players to the game.

Moving at Digital Speed: The Key to Value Innovation

Change creates opportunities for value innovation. Given advancements in technology, many industries are changing at lightning speed. The faster change occurs, the more important speed becomes. Not surprisingly, business models have to shift at astronomical rates. The emergence of the Internet, additional improvements in telecommunications, access to such new markets as Eastern Europe, Russia, and China, and advancements in idea creation have all led to significant change in a relatively short period of time.

> Growth champions have the attitude that you must keep moving or get out of the way.

Change encourages the emergence of new opportunities. Opportunities create growth. The companies that are quickest to exploit change are the companies that win. *Speed is critical for value innovation.*

In a recent article discussing the new realities of strategy and growth, Dr. Peter Lorange, president of the International Institute of Management Development, contends that one of the biggest inhibitors to growth is lack of speed.[2] Speed is the enabler of value innovation. The faster a company can commercialize a new product or service, the larger the impact of the value innovation. Moving quickly to get a new product to market can provide such benefits as an increased customer base and enhanced brand loyalty. One of the founding editors of *Fast Company,* Alan Webber, recently stated: "An organization that eliminates wasted time in manufacturing, services, new product development, and sales and distribution will cut costs, service customers better, reduce inventories, and enhance innovation."[3]

Doing business on a digital playing field has truly created a new business model. While we are inundated with success stories of companies selling products over the Internet, significant benefits also accrue to organizations that use electronic processes to increase overall company performance. E-business is much more than e-tailing. Use of the Internet and Web as communication media have also had a significant impact on the ability of companies to increase their speed in commercializing value innovations. Improved inventory management, changing distribution systems, and increasing the speed of getting new products to market are being realized by numerous companies in almost every industry.

Information technology and the rapid development of the Internet have raised the bar in terms of the impact of speed on value innovation. E-business revolutionized the way Dell Computers approached supply chain management. A critical driver for Dell's customers was speed of delivery. In response, Dell decided to change its business model. Today, customers can visit Dell's Web site and design their own computers; and Dell can manufacture, ship, and deliver the product by the next business day. How has Dell so dramatically increased its speed? By using the Internet. Dell has strategically located all of its suppliers within 15 minutes of its factory. Warehousing is outsourced so Dell carries no inventory. All companies are electronically linked to supercharge information flows, but for distribution, Dell has partnered with UPS, which acts as a logistics manager. UPS inventories various types of monitors and then matches the correct monitor with the correct computer and delivers the final system to the customer.

Although Dell has used the Internet between companies to improve its speed, speed in value innovation can also be enhanced by sharing information between different groups within the same organization via *intranet* technology. Hewlett-Packard (H-P) has been successful in innovating value because of its strong communication between its marketing, product research, and operations departments. Using intranet technology has greatly enhanced the ability of the groups to interact and communicate with each other, thereby improving H-P's speed in getting new value innovations commercialized.

Admittedly, technology has also simplified purchasing for consumers by affecting the speed with which customers can shop. Customers can get product specifications and third-party product performance evaluations as well as compare competitors' products with just a click of a mouse. As consumers are becoming more comfortable purchasing over the Internet, the basic philosophy of retailing is dramatically changing. Aggressive, quick movers know how important speed is. The first companies to capitalize on some of these technology innovations (e.g., simplifying purchasing decisions for customers using Internet technology) are reaping huge rewards.

Defining the Game: Getting a Bigger Piece of the Pie versus Making the Pie Bigger

Most companies follow traditional strategic thinking. Consequently, they don't innovate value and thus most will never sustain significant growth. I challenge conventional strategic thought. Emphasis in traditional strategic thought is on understanding our competitive markets so that markets are defined by competition or products. When we see ourselves through our competitors, our markets are defined by standard industrial classification (SIC) codes or, more recently, the North American industry classification system (NAICS) rather than by customers' values and needs. Defining markets based on artificial boundaries such as classification codes limits growth opportunities. Growth champions don't constrain their markets by using these arbitrary boundaries. Growth champions develop an intimate understanding of their customers' needs, which often results in value innovation.

Growth champions successfully break away from the constraints imposed by traditional strategic thought. Rather than following the leader, as most companies do, growth companies sustain growth year after year by identifying opportunities that others don't see. They figure out better ways to serve their customers. Growth champions do not, however, search for just any opportunity. Growing for the sake of growth is dangerous. Over time, companies that try to be all things to all people, pursing growth opportunities just to make a quick buck, will lose. Dell Computer Corporation has embraced this notion to become a textbook example of a growth champion. Over the past decade, Dell has identified numerous growth opportunities, but the company will not simply pursue a growth opportunity just for the sake of growth. Michael Dell positions his company to be aggressive but only to the extent that a new growth opportunity makes strategic sense. "We look aggressively for add-on businesses," he states. "This does not mean wild diversification. Our focus is on clearly connected businesses. We have developed services that our customers wanted, such as selling peripherals in software, integration services, financial services. It's a logical progression strategy."[4]

How do you know what types of growth opportunities are right for your business? Which ones make the most sense? How can a company balance the risks associated with pursuing new opportunities to sustain growth? Growth opportunities come in two different forms: *incremental growth* and *leap growth*. Sustainable growth occurs by achieving a balance between these two types of opportunities. How do growth champions frame their markets using incremental and leap growth? Let's begin with a brief discussion of the fundamental differences between incremental and leap-growth opportunities.

- *Incremental-growth opportunities* result from minor improvements to something a company already does. Incremental growth often follows the traditional view of strategy by focusing on competition in a well-defined industry. This type of growth is achieved by gaining market share, focusing on getting a bigger piece of the pie. For one company to get a bigger piece of the pie, a competitor has to give it up. So unless your industry is growing at a rapid pace, a traditional view of strategy will lead only to incremental growth. If a company continually focuses on getting a bigger piece of the pie, sooner or later it will hit a wall. Many average companies limit themselves by their self-imposed definition of a competitive market— by the size of their pie. In contrast, growth champions don't limit themselves to artificial, predetermined constraints (a.k.a. market boundaries).

- *Leap-growth opportunities* result from value innovation and are often radical, challenging conventional strategic thought. Leap growth usually results from a company's emphasis on value to satisfy current and future needs of customers. This type of growth focuses on *expanding the pie* to allow significant growth. Rarely does leap growth result from focusing on competition. Growth companies know that the only way to achieve significant growth over the long term is to expand their pie. Rather than exhausting all of their energy on stealing away incremental market share from competitors, fast-growth companies figure out ways to make the pie bigger. The larger the pie becomes, the greater the growth opportunities.

Growth companies are well aware that these two types of growth opportunities exist. Here's a key attribute that separates growth champions from ordinary companies:

*O*rdinary companies race to beat competition.
    Fast-growth companies race to beat customers' expectations.

Obviously, leap-growth opportunities are more difficult to pursue compared with incremental-growth opportunities. They are often controversial and somewhat elusive to most businesses, so more risk is associated with leap-growth opportunities.

Effective growth companies find a balance between incremental-growth and leap-growth opportunities. Incremental growth provides consistency and stability. Leap growth is much riskier, but the rewards are much greater. If a company pursues incremental growth only, it will usually move along at a slow, steady pace, never becoming better than average. If a company pursues leap-growth opportunities only, it may become a one-hit wonder, quickly rising to the top of the charts, only to disappear a short time later. Given the risks and capital requirements associated with leap growth, seldom is a company successful without maintaining a balance between incremental growth and leap growth. In Chapter 6, I discuss numerous strategies for pursuing both types of growth and why growth champions have the consistency of the tortoise and the speed of the hare.

External Framing: The Essence of Growth

Most managers would agree that it is better to have an outside-in perspective than an inside-out one. Numerous consultants suggest that successful companies have to look at themselves as an outsider would to understand customers' needs. Admittedly, looking at a company from the outside in is important. It provides managers with new ways to look at old problems, but it simply isn't good enough anymore because the rules have changed. Looking from the outside in makes a company reactive to market demands. To innovate value, however, a company must stay ahead of customers, not competitors, and an outside-in perspective, by itself, just doesn't cut it anymore.

The whole idea of having an inside-out perspective seems to be a thing of the past. Traditionally, thinking from the inside out meant that managers would flip up their blinders, focusing internally on their products and operations while ignoring such outside factors as customer needs and market demands. Therefore, today most managers would agree that thinking from the inside out only encourages counterproductivity. Before you decide to lay the idea of an inside-out perspective to rest, consider the fact that many growth champions use an inside-out perspective to catapult their way to the top.

A winning inside-out perspective does originate internally, but it is not internally focused. Rather than focusing on tangible resources (e.g., products) this new type of inside-out perspective focuses on such intangible resources as the accumulation of intellectual property, leading-edge managerial knowledge, and superior technological expertise. Developing this type of knowledge evolves over time; it is the essence of a learning organization. Growth companies educate themselves better than anyone else in terms of value. As a result, they understand better than anyone else how to satisfy their customers' current needs as well as their future needs. This new rendition of the inside-out perspective allows companies to anticipate customer needs rather than just keep pace with them.

Growth champions achieve success by balancing an effective outside-in perspective with their new definition of an inside-out perspective. In contrast with most average companies, it's much more than merely taking an outside-in view. Growth-oriented companies are able to look at themselves as a customer views them (from the outside in), but they also know their business better than anyone else (from the inside out). They supercharge their outside-in knowledge with appropriate inside-out knowledge—an unparalleled level of expertise. This internally generated expertise comes in many forms. Having a leading-edge understanding of technology allows a company to anticipate customer needs. Expertise in product applications, unique distribution channels, quality management, employee motivation, and action planning can be combined with an outside-in perspective to put a company ahead of the pack.

It is the combination of these two factors—looking at your company from the outside in combined with leading-edge expertise—that allows a company to provide value to its markets better than anyone else. Moreover, these two factors feed off each other; growth champions don't try to separate them. As a company learns something about a market, managers can use the information to develop appropriate expertise. Conversely, as a company develops leading-edge expertise, it may provide managers with a new platform to view their markets in ways that customers haven't even begun to think about yet. The result: growth champions are continuously identifying opportunities that most companies will never see. The ability to combine these two thought processes is what I call *external framing* as seen in Figure 2.1. This is a critical key to sustainable growth—the underlying essence that makes a growth champion.

By using external framing, managers pay little attention to organizational boundaries and, to some extent, pay little attention to market boundaries. Instead of making competition their focal point, they focus on value innovation. Instead of focusing on efficiencies, they focus on effectiveness. Through external framing, managers often understand customers' needs better than customers do.

> *R*ather than thinking *like* customers, external framing gives managers the ability to think *for* customers.

That's what allows successful growth companies to offer products and services that fulfill needs customers haven't even thought of yet.

FIGURE 2.1   External Framing: Anticipating Value

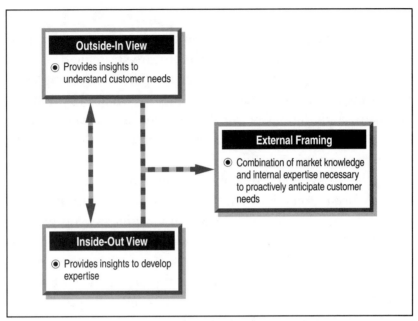

Taking a Good Look at Yourself

External framing is critical to attain and sustain growth. Almost every company has some unique knowledge base. Once you begin to understand what drives value in your markets, combine your own expertise with your market knowledge. This will lead you down the path to external framing—and it all starts with something as simple as how you view yourself. What is your company all about? What is the underlying reason for your company's existence (other than maximizing shareholder wealth)? Defining why your company exists can be the difference between developing an external framework or remaining part of the average crowd. You basically have two choices:

1. You can view your company through the products or services you offer.

2. You can view your company through the value you create and provide.

Something as elementary as how you view your own company will dramatically influence its future strategic direction. Numerous examples can be found of companies that completely change their focus (and ultimately their performance) by rethinking the underlying reason for their existence and taking a new look at themselves. IBM and Smith Corona were fierce competitors in the typewriter industry. Smith Corona viewed itself by its products: typewriters; IBM viewed itself by the value it provided: office automation. The result is clear. As computer technology evolved, managers at Smith Corona saw no growth opportunities—they were a typewriter manufacturer. In contrast, managers at IBM saw a tremendous opportunity to improve value. Two similar companies in the same situation and two different outcomes based on each company's self-perception.

The classic example to illustrate the power of defining your business based on value instead of products is railroad companies in the early 1900s. If you had asked a president of one of the major railroads what business he was in, he would have replied, "We are in the railroad business, of course!" These companies defined themselves by focusing on the products or services they offered. From an external-framing viewpoint, it is clear that railroad companies provided value via transportation. Value came from moving people and cargo from one location to another. Needless to say, as highway trucking increased and airplane technology evolved, the major railroads put on their proverbial blinders and looked the other way. It wasn't part of their business; from a traditional perspective, they were in the railroad business. If these companies would have used external framing, they would have seen that trucks and airplanes were natural extensions of their business—tremendous growth opportunities. Did they have the money to invest in alternative modes of transportation? Absolutely. Railroads were among the most powerful and profitable businesses in the world at that time. Had they used external framing, they would probably again be among the largest corporations in the world today. Instead, most railroads went bankrupt and, for the most part, the remaining players in the industry today are struggling to survive. Yes, something as simple as how you view yourself is the first step to externally framing your markets, and external framing provides companies with limitless opportunities for growth.

Efficiency versus Effectiveness: Doing Things Right versus Doing the Right Thing

Numerous benefits result from external framing. Knowing the difference between efficiency and effectiveness is at the heart of these benefits and is critical to growth champions. What is the difference between efficiency and effectiveness? Efficiency often ignores the outside environment; the primary unit of analysis is the company itself. Conversely, when a company focuses on effectiveness, it views itself as a small part of a greater whole, as a single piece of the puzzle. The unit of analysis is the market, not the company. Simply stated, efficiency and effectiveness are two opposite ways of looking at the world.

Efficiency focuses on doing things right. It is an internally driven perspective that ignores external factors. It focuses on trying to improve something you currently do, usually in the area of operations. *Effectiveness* focuses on doing the right thing and is a natural extension of external framing. Effectiveness can be assessed by considering three critical questions:

1. Who are our customers?

2. What value do we currently provide?

3. What needs are emerging?

Who are our customers? This question may seem easy to answer, but don't shortchange yourself. In many cases it is quite clear who your customers are. In other cases it might not be as apparent. Recently, I was working with a group at Caterpillar and we spent an entire day trying to define its customers. We considered other groups within the company that used its products, dealers that sold the products, purchasing agents who bought the products from dealers, and end users of the products. Each of the numerous constituencies had a different set of needs.

Who are your customers? Is it as simple as defining the end user? Is it the person who cuts the check? Sometimes the answers are clear, other times difficult. Note that identifying your customer(s) is only a starting point, not the final destination. You need to know your markets to understand value.

What value do we currently provide? Many average companies consider themselves externally framed, looking at themselves from the customer's point of view. As previously discussed, focusing on the customer isn't good enough. Instead, focus on the needs that your company fulfills—the value your company provides. Focusing on customers can limit growth potential. Focusing on value, on the other hand, can open the door to many opportunities for achieving fast and sustainable growth. The difference between focusing on customers and focusing on value may seem subtle, but it is just such subtle differences that separate average companies from growth champions.

What needs are emerging? Many average companies are satisfied if they can get a pulse on their customers' current needs. This is not the way a growth champion thinks; growth champions are far ahead of the pack. They lead the pack by anticipating customers' needs before customers even know these needs exist. Value innovations like 3Com's Palm Pilot and Federal Express's hub-and-spoke overnight delivery system literally *created* needs to achieve growth. Proactive managers look to the future and anticipate and plan for change. One reason for emphasizing external framing so strongly is that it helps a business to develop a proactive rather than a reactive style of management. Proactive managers see opportunities on the horizon and position their business to benefit from them. Michael Dell recently stated:

> We strive to be out in front of key trends in our business to gain a greater share of a faster-growing market. The Internet is one example. We know that virtually everybody is going to buy their computer over the Internet in five to ten years. We want to dominate that market and have a leadership position in sales of computers through new distribution channels.[5]

Dell Computer Corporation isn't sitting back enjoying its current success. The company is proactively positioning itself for future trends, anticipating customers' needs before the customers are aware the needs exist. In contrast, a reactive business is driven by day-to-day demands. Events occur and the firm responds. It is usually undergoing new, usually unanticipated, traumas. Crisis management is the modus operandi, and putting out the largest fire is the focus of most activity. In all likelihood, the business that fails to recognize and analyze its environment will fall victim to change.

The efficiency versus effectiveness argument seems basic, but many managers don't understand why it's more important to be doing the right thing (effectiveness) than doing things right (efficiency). A company can be very efficient at something, but if it doesn't generate value as defined by the market, then the efficiency not only wastes resources on something that doesn't matter but actually destroys value. It's a zero-sum situation—investing in an efficiency that doesn't add value means you're taking away resources that could be invested in a value innovation activity.

Some companies are so inwardly focused and so worried about maximizing efficiencies that they never step back to see the big picture—seeing if they are doing the right thing. For example, I was working with a company a couple of years ago that was boasting it had the best customer service in its industry. They bragged: "We invest about $10 million in customer service systems every year . . . twice as much as the next competitor!" As it turns out, customers in that industry didn't care at all about customer service. They said their most important purchasing driver was price. Here was a company that had a very efficient customer service program in place. Managers at the company were proud of the investment they had made to provide great after-sales service. Unfortunately, they never took the time to ask their customers what was important. The managers were so concerned with efficiencies that they never stopped to see if they were effective. They were so focused on doing things right that they never realized they were not doing the right things. Customers were concerned with price, but the company was investing millions a year on something that customers didn't even care about—driving the cost base up with each dollar spent on customer service.

For companies that are fortunate to be doing the right thing, efficiency may not even be a necessity (at least in the short run). Have you ever known entrepreneurs that made money in spite of themselves? They were doing the right thing—providing value to customers. I recently ran across an individual who had previously been employed as a research engineer. He is a brilliant designer of network software but has poor business skills. A couple of years ago, he set off on his own. He started out with five employees and, after a few months of operation, he had to hire another ten. Revenues in his first year of operation exceeded $3 million. He kept expanding, the entire time becoming more and more inefficient. Projects were behind schedule. No project management system was in place—sure disaster for a research design company, right? Fortunately for this company, it was effective—it was doing the right thing albeit not efficiently. Demand was so high for the company's services that it could get away with inefficiencies. It has a weak marketing department, it doesn't manage operations well, and it continues to grow. Why? Because there is such a high demand for its services. This company is successful in spite of itself because it's doing the right thing. Admittedly, as more competitors enter the market or when the market slows down, weaker players will be squeezed out. So eventually this company must improve its efficiencies.

What important lesson do we learn from all of this? Clearly, it's more important to be effective first.

> Once you know you are *doing the right thing,* then start figuring out ways *to do things right.*

First comes effectiveness, then efficiency. Companies that use external framing already know this. It's much better to be the effective software developer that needs to ramp up efficiencies rather than the manufacturer with a very efficient customer service department when customers don't care about after-sales service.

Unfortunately, most managers choose (yes, choose!) to look at the world from an efficiency point of view. This is the way it's been done in the past; it's a controlled environment; it's comfortable and settled. Growth champions break out of that mold; they don't believe if it isn't broken, don't fix it. Change is the rule and they actively seek opportunities for growth.

Mining for Diamonds

As we have already learned, growth champions are good at using an outside-in approach *and* an inside-out approach. It is not good enough to think like customers anymore (the outside-in approach). Any company can *think* like customers. It is simply a matter of asking customers what they think. *Understanding* what customers need is a whole different animal. It is the difference between thinking *for* customers and thinking *like* customers. It is the difference between *meeting* customer expectations and *exceeding* customer expectations.

The title of this section is based on a story told by Russell Herman Conwell back in the 1870s. Dr. Conwell wanted to raise money to found a new university. He toured the country, giving more than 6,000 lectures, and in each one he told a story called "Acres of Diamonds." The story had such a dramatic impact on his audiences that Dr. Conwell raised enough money to found Temple University. This same story appeared many years later in Earl Nightingale's best-seller *Lead the Field.* It's a true story that has a powerful message, a message that captures the critical necessity of having both an outside-in and an inside-out perspective for developing a solid external frame.

Dr. Conwell's story is about an African farmer who had heard numerous stories of other African farmers making millions of dollars by discovering diamond mines. The stories captivated the farmer so much that he sold his farm to find a diamond mine himself but spent the rest of his life aimlessly wandering the African continent in search of hitting it big—finding a diamond mine that would make him rich beyond his wildest dreams. As the story goes, eventually the farmer became so frustrated and worn out that he threw himself into a river and drowned.

Meanwhile, the man who bought his farm was crossing a small stream on the property when he saw a bright burst of color coming from the bottom of the stream. He knelt down and picked up a stone. Admiring its beauty, he put it in his pocket and later that day placed it up on the fireplace mantel in his home. A few weeks later, a friend stopped by to visit and noticed the sparkling stone on the mantel. After carefully examining the stone, the friend asked the farmer if he knew what he had found. The farmer replied that he thought it was a pretty piece of crystal. The friend informed the farmer that he had found one of the biggest diamonds ever discovered. The farmer couldn't believe what he was hearing. He informed the man that there were many more stones just like it in the creek, maybe not as large as the one on the mantel, but there was an abundance of these stones in the creek.

Needless to say, this same farm that the first farmer was so anxious to sell to find a diamond mine turned out to be the most productive diamond mine in all of Africa. The first farmer had owned—outright—acres of diamonds, but he sold them for virtually nothing to look for them elsewhere. The opportunity was staring him in the eye but he just never saw it. If the farmer had only taken the time to educate himself—to study what a diamond looked like in its rough form—he would have achieved his dream. He should have explored his own farm before looking elsewhere. The underlying message that Dr. Conwell emphasized is that we are all standing in the middle of our own acres of diamonds.

So why is it that growth companies excel and average companies remain average? Average companies and growth companies, when faced with the same situation, perceive their environments in very different ways. Where an average company may see a stagnant industry, a growth company will effectively explore the market, looking for opportunities that most others will never see. Only by having knowledge and patience does a growth company uncover opportunities that would have gone unnoticed by most. Growth companies are constantly learning, educating themselves to know what their diamonds look like in rough form.

We must continue to explore, to continually attempt to find new ideas. In the end, we may realize that some of our greatest opportunities were right under our noses the entire time. Therefore, it may prove fruitful to look in your own backyard before venturing out of the neighborhood to find new and exciting growth opportunities. For example, Netscape has gotten too far ahead of the rest of the industry on occasion, looking for highly creative ways to grow when bigger and better opportunities were literally just sitting there, waiting to be picked up. In 1995, Netscape aggressively pursued Java programming. The company invested considerable resources in Java-based development only to realize that the language was too immature to meet Netscape's needs. By looking too far into the future, Marc Andreessen missed some diamonds in his own backyard. In 1998, Andreessen admitted that he let a major opportunity slip through his hands:

> I thought [using our Web site] was a distraction. It's kind of funny to think about how many people have had the opportunity to make billion-dollar mistakes. I absolutely thought we were a software company—we build software and put it in boxes, and we sell it. Oops. Wrong.[6]

Anticipating change is extremely difficult, if not impossible. Proactive companies make mistakes all the time. But in the long run, it's the proactive company that will succeed, leaving reactive companies in the dust. Proactiveness, however, starts in your own backyard.

Life Cycle Traps: The Danger of Off-the-Shelf Models

Managers of typical companies often try to define their markets by forcing them into widely accepted models. Off-the-shelf models are everywhere. The most popular come in the life cycle variety: company life cycles, product life cycles, and industry life cycles. I don't believe in life cycles. Neither do the leaders of fast-growth businesses. Life cycle models only constrain businesses, and most life cycle theories used in business applications are merely a trap. Think about it: if you follow a life cycle mentality, you end up with death. Rather than life cycles, we should call them death cycles because they lead to maturity and death.

In 1959, Edith Penrose, author of the *Theory of Growth of the Firm,* contended that physical science models have no place in such social sciences as business. Physical science models work fine in a black-and-white world—any living organism on Earth is born, grows, matures, and eventually dies. That's a law of nature, part of the physical sciences. Although physical science models may work fine in explaining the life cycles of living organisms, business is much more complex in predicting stages. The social sciences are not so black and white—they fall into a gray category. Why? Businesses are made up of people, individuals with different personalities, even changing personalities. And we all have different ways of looking at the world—our perceptions are unique to each of us. Consequently, we all have different attitudes.

Business literature is full of life cycle models, each of which claims to show a predictable pattern from birth through death. Forget about them. When a growth business hits the mature phase, do you think its leaders sit back and wait for the company to die? No! Quite often they try to break out of traditional life cycle models, finding new uses for their products or services. They try to take their business out of the mature stage and move it back into the growth stage.

Ask the management at Arm & Hammer, makers of baking soda, if they believe in life cycles. The baking soda industry had been mature for decades and arguably was decaying and dying. Then it was discovered that baking soda was very effective at absorbing odors. People started buying boxes of baking soda to put into their refrigerators and freezers to absorb those nasty odors we are all too familiar with. Because baking soda was effective at absorbing odors, Arm & Hammer expanded into almost every industry where odor absorption was important: laundry detergents, carpet cleaners, toothpaste, and body deodorants. A company, a product, and an industry that were in their final stages of the life cycle model suddenly became hot. The odor absorption market realized significant growth when Arm & Hammer entered center stage and became the biggest winner of all. The company realized record growth because of baking soda's newfound uses.

No provision in the life cycle model is made for this type of behavior. Unfortunately, the life cycle model, which predicts where we are and where we are going, is too simplistic for the complex environment of business growth. Businesses are not that predictable. And businesses have the ability to reverse stages in the life cycle. A life cycle mentality will only constrain you and discourage growth for your business. Many companies are hurt or artificially constrained because they allow themselves to be pigeonholed into a life cycle mentality.

Instead of completely disregarding life cycles, be aware of their limitations. In his *Harvard Business Review* classic, author Larry Greiner provides useful advice for using life cycle models.[7] A company in a certain stage of the life cycle must be aware of specific challenges. Every business is in one stage of the life cycle model at any given moment, and must face issues unique to that stage. There is a benefit to considering the stages in the life cycle as long as you consider the stages independent of each other. The danger of a life cycle model is when a business leader uses the model as a scientist would.

Just because your business is in a growth stage doesn't mean you have to settle on maturity in the near future. There are companies, maybe even companies in your industry, that enjoy sustainable growth. Don't regress to that tired old excuse that we can't grow because we're in a mature market. There are companies in almost every mature market that manage to grow faster than their industries.

Identifying Value Drivers

In this chapter I've talked about several different approaches growth champions use to view themselves and their markets. But how do they use all of this information to make decisions? How do they turn all of this information into bottom-line growth and profitability?

Growth champions have the ability to understand what truly drives value in their markets. They don't limit their focus to products; they don't limit their focus to markets. They focus on value. Rather than looking at markets in terms of conventional strategic thought—competition—growth champions frame their markets externally, using their expertise to figure out new ways to innovate value for customers. Rather than focusing exclusively on getting a bigger piece of the pie, they focus on making the pie bigger.

Without a solid understanding of market drivers, it is virtually impossible for a company to innovate value, to be a market driver. The ultimate goal of effective external framing is to identify the major underlying drivers for the industry. The key word here is *major*. Quite often managers use a shotgun approach in an attempt to cover everything under the sun as a possible driver because they are unsure what drives value. Some drivers may be extremely important to determining the future of the industry and others may have minimal impact. Growth champions are very astute at differentiating underlying value drivers from the consequences of these drivers.

Endnotes

1. W. Chan Kim and Renee Mauborgne, "Value Innovation: The Strategic Logic of High Growth," *Harvard Business Review* 75 (January-February 1997): 103–12.

2. Peter Lorange, "Strategy Implementation: The New Realities," *Long Range Planning* 31, no. 1 (1998): 18–29.

3. Alan M. Webber, "Are You on Digital Time?" *Fast Company* 22 (1999): 114–19.

4. Michael Dell, "Maximum Speed," *Executive Excellence* 16, no. 1 (1999): 15–16.

5. Ibid.

6. David B. Yoffie and Michael A. Cusumano, "Building a Company on Internet Time: Lessons from Netscape" *California Management Review* 41, no. 3 (Spring 1999): 8–28.

7. Larry E. Greiner, "Revolution as Organizations Grow," *Harvard Business Review* (reprint HBR Classic) (May-June 1998): 55–67.

Firing Up the Growth Engine

How to Identify Great Growth Opportunities

*O*ften in executive development seminars, I'll stand up in front of an audience and pose a straightforward question: "How do you grow a business?" Answers start coming from all over the room and inevitably the participants end up in a competitive state of mind. "Cut price to increase market share," they'll say, or "Increase advertising to differentiate products from competitors." They put on their blinders and erect their artificial walls. It's safe and comfortable in well-defined four-digit SIC environments, safe from all outside elements.

Then there is always someone in the room, probably someone that has recently met with a management consultant, who confidently blurts out, "To grow you must think outside the box." Everyone simultaneously nods in approval as if they had just heard the carnal truth. I'll innocently respond, "What box?" The audience is silent.

Thinking outside the box sounds provocative, but it has no substance. This elusive box could represent our current product line, our company boundaries, or maybe our industry boundaries—all arbitrary designations. How can you think outside the box if you don't know what the box is? Let me play devil's advocate for a moment. I say to grow, a company must think inside the box . . . the right box, the effective box—a box that provides management with an external frame so that value innovation rather than competition becomes the focal point. Thinking outside the box, in a sense, suggests that there are certain areas that a company should *not* focus on but, unfortunately, provides little direction for what the company *should* focus on. And while competition does have its place (I'll talk about that in Part III), many executives don't comprehend that to achieve *sustainable* growth, a company must continually generate new growth opportunities through an externally framed view of the world.

To identify fast-growth opportunities, not only do you need the right frame of mind but you need to know where to look. But what do growth opportunities look like? If there are an infinite number of growth opportunities out there, how do we see them? Where do we start?

In the last chapter I talked about the importance of developing an external frame as a new way of viewing your markets. External framing should give you a good idea *why* firms grow. This chapter will focus on *how* they grow—that is, on identifying and exploiting growth opportunities. How a company views its markets is intimately related to its ability to identify growth opportunities. And the payoff for effectively framing your markets externally is continuous growth opportunities regardless of the business you're in or your industry. As marketing guru Theodore Levitt points out in *Harvard Business Review*, "In truth there is no such thing as a growth industry . . . there are only companies organized and operated to create and capitalize on growth opportunities." As we see in this chapter, growth opportunities are everywhere: growth markets and stagnant markets, manufacturing sectors and service sectors, high-tech industries and low-tech industries—they are everywhere if you know where to look for them.

FIGURE 3.1   The Four Ps of Opportunity Identification

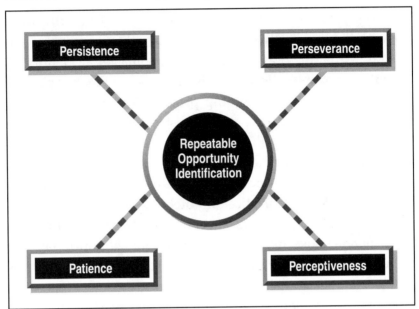

Using External Framing as a Platform: The Four Ps of Opportunity Identification

Having an external frame is a starting point, but it's the means, not the end. I imagine numerous companies have a solid external frame but remain average for a variety of reasons: a culture that discourages growth, managers who avoid risk, or an organization's inability to embrace change and take action. External framing provides a platform in which managers can begin to identify growth opportunities. To achieve fast and sustainable growth, managers must sharpen their focus to identify business opportunities that are not obvious to everyone else. Extending the external framing platform into a repeatable process for opportunity identification requires commitment at many levels. Figure 3.1 shows four qualities of growth champions that allow them to be masters of opportunity identification.

Persistence

Many managers believe that opportunity identification takes place periodically when the time is right. Growth champions know that the only way to become a master at identifying growth opportunities is to relentlessly persist, to make opportunity identification an ongoing process. To accomplish this, growth champions realize that almost everything is a learning opportunity. Consider Richard Branson, the risk-seeking chairman and president of the Virgin Group, who sees opportunities that most others in his position would never see. His secret: he carries with him a collection of notebooks in which he writes down his observations and ideas on a daily basis. In his hundreds of notebooks, his observations turn into opportunities that were just out there waiting to happen. An observant manager is one who is constantly learning, constantly thinking of new ways to grow. Conversely, a manager who just goes through the motions may have a gold mine (or diamond mine) right under his or her nose but never knows it's there. Observation leads to fresh ideas, contacts, and opportunities; and it all starts with opening your eyes.

Patience

Rarely will opportunities just jump into your lap; it takes time to identify opportunities and growth champions are very patient about this identification process. They know you must be pragmatic and take it one step at a time. Trying to force opportunity identification is usually counterproductive. When I lecture to executives about effective negotiation, I tell them that one of the most important attributes I have observed in excellent negotiators is their patience in letting "the game" come to them. They don't force things unless their backs are against the wall, which holds true for opportunity identification. Many times, it's beneficial to let the game come to you rather than forcing your company to meet some unrealistic metric (e.g., promising to identify at least one new growth opportunity each month).

Perseverance

Identifying growth opportunities requires a lot of work. Inevitably, you'll hit some dead ends and become frustrated, but what separates growth champions from ordinary companies is:

> *W*here ordinary companies give up and regress to blaming markets for their misfortunes, growth champions persevere.

Tom Peters, well-known management expert, stresses the importance of perseverance by advising that rather than giving up and coming away empty-handed from an effort to look for new ideas, managers should systematically record their findings. "Recording what you see teaches you another critical project lesson: Little things do matter."[1] As we have already discussed, subtle differences between value creation and value innovation, being market driven versus being a market driver, and thinking for customers rather than thinking like customers, are the indiscernible differences that separate an ordinary company from an extraordinary company.

Perceptiveness

Perceptiveness is also a critical factor in determining a company's ability to identify new opportunities. Why does one company perceive a growth opportunity while another company doesn't? Does the difference stem from unparalleled creativity or basic common sense? Actually, perceptiveness is often the result of a combination of creativity and common sense.

Much is written about creativity, but little about common sense. We automatically assume that to be able to perceive opportunities that others can't see, we need to be a creative genius. Creativity is often important, but many times common sense should dictate. Sam Walton didn't achieve success through extraordinary creativity; he achieved it through basic common sense. He realized that consumers in medium-sized cities had some of the same retailing needs as consumers in large metropolitan areas.

Even though change is occurring at astronomical rates, many commonsense business principles that have stood the test of time continue to apply—for example, serve the customer better than anyone else serves the customer. Sometimes such a principle may require creativity but more often is just a matter of common sense.

The End of the Rainbow: Where to Look for Fast-Growth Opportunities

Fast-growth opportunities are everywhere. With the right mind-set and an effective understanding of where these opportunities lurk, any company can develop the ability to identify fast-growth opportunities. Unfortunately, there is no easy way to see what others don't see. Moreover, not all fast-growth opportunities look the same. The good news is that we can categorize most fast-growth opportunities into one of four types (as seen in Figure 3.2), and recognizing and understanding these categories provide a starting point for developing the ability to see great opportunities.

FIGURE 3.2   Forms of Fast Growth

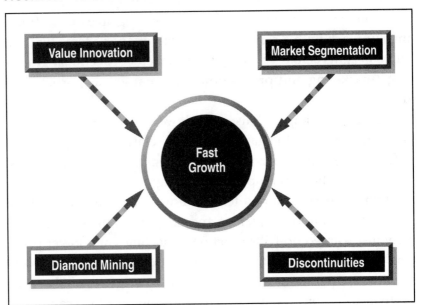

Value Innovation

In *Business Week*'s 1999 list of hot growth companies, Amy Barrett summed up the winners by stating that "[w]hether they are apparel makers or semiconductor manufacturers, this year's winners have an uncanny ability to spot what their customers want next." Companies that can understand value innovation and fulfill customer needs proactively can ride the growth wave in a "winner takes all" scenario.

What does it take to anticipate customers' needs (not wants)? The systems that growth champions use vary as much as the opportunities themselves. For some, a formalized environmental scanning system may work best, one that specifically relies on published data. For others, it may be a highly advanced customer insight technology such as data warehousing and data mining. Still others do it the old-fashioned way by asking the customers, whether in small focus groups, interviews, or widely distributed surveys. A best-case scenario is to use all of these techniques. Ideally, managers should develop an organization that understands market trends by combining an external framing approach with a companywide network of systems that can share insights across various groups, whether functional groups (e.g., marketing and production), regional groups, or product divisions.

In the last chapter, I discussed how Compaq almost crashed by playing the me-too game with IBM. Only after management refocused on value innovation and began to understand customer needs did the company realize significant and sustainable growth. In 1991, Compaq felt there were customers out there who didn't want more gizmos and gadgets on their computers: they just wanted no-frills functional machines at a lower price. Unfortunately, the company was not designed for low-cost machines. Operations were not set up to manage cost and neither were distribution systems. So what did Compaq do to capture its redefined definition of value in the PC market? The company literally reinvented itself. In a matter of a few months, Compaq increased its distribution from 3,000 dealers to over 30,000 retailers, including mass retailers such as Circuit City and Wal-Mart. By seeing an opportunity that others didn't see—low-end computers—Compaq increased its revenues from $3 billion to over $25 billion in less than six years and today is a world leader in desktop computers, portables, servers, and workstations. In terms of value innovation, Eckhard Pfeiffer, Compaq's former CEO, "clearly articulated and never wavered from his intention to value innovate."[2] It was Compaq's ability to understand value and then position itself to exploit value innovation that propelled the company to the top.

Accor, a company that literally redefined the French budget hotel industry, is another example of a business that identified a growth opportunity by understanding value. Accor's approach was based on commonsense questions—questions that a lot of companies can use to understand value in their own markets:

- *What basic factors did the industry take for granted?* In the budget hotel industry, it was the ability to offer a comfortable night's sleep.

- *Did these assumptions actually deliver fundamental value to customers?* One of the underlying assumptions in the market was that a low price for a hotel room meant that customers would get an uncomfortable bed and a lot of noise. Given that customers stayed at hotels to get a good night's sleep, the industry's assumption (completely accepted by customers) did not deliver value.

- *What did the industry offer that customers didn't need and that didn't provide significant value?* In France, even most budget hotels provided expensive restaurants, fancy lounges, and full-service reception desks (e.g., concierge services and bell captains).

- *What did customers want (i.e., how did they define value) that wasn't being offered?* Customers staying at budget hotels basically wanted to get a good night's sleep at a fair price.

- *What did customers need that the industry had never thought of before?* Inexpensive rooms that still allowed customers to get a good night's sleep was what customers needed (and wanted).

Accor decided to eliminate expensive restaurants, fancy lounges, and full-service reception desks. Moreover, except during peak hours, the reception desks weren't even staffed— everything was automated. In addition, amenities such as complimentary stationery, desks, and decorations were not included in the rooms. What customers could expect was to get a good night's sleep in a high-quality comfortable bed without a lot of noise. Given the tremendous cost reductions realized from Accor's elimination of nonvalue-serving amenities, the company was able to offer rooms (with five-star beds) starting at about 60 French francs per night.

The result, in the budget hotel industry (which most contended was suffering from overcapacity resulting in severe stagnation), Accor shot straight to the top, owning more market share than its next five competitors—combined. Could Accor have realized this success by focusing on competitors? Obviously, Accor's success has come from value innovation—seeing opportunities that no one else saw by understanding value.

Diamond Mining

Recall Herman Conwell's story of the African farmer in the previous chapter. Conwell's basic message was that the greatest opportunities available to most people (and most companies) are right under their feet. Right now, at this very moment, your company is sitting in the middle of acres of diamonds. Look around; there's probably a very good reason why you are doing what you're doing. At some point your company made a conscious decision to pursue the line of work you are currently in. Why was that?

Before a consultant advises you to wildly diversify into new industries in search of new growth opportunities and greener pastures, make sure that your current pasture is not just as green . . . or even greener. As Earl Nightingale observed in *Lead the Field*, "It's been said that if the other guy's pasture appears to be greener than ours, it's quite possible that it's getting better care. Besides, while we're looking at other pastures, other people are looking at ours!"

The big growth opportunity that you've always been looking for may have been right in front of you all the time. Here's another true story to illustrate the importance of ensuring that you understand the opportunities that surround you before set-ting sail to find other opportunities. During the Great Depres-sion, people in every walk of life were devastated. West Texas was no different than any other region. The Tate family was des-titute, living off of welfare as many families had to do. They lived on a small ranch that the family had owned for some time. When the depression was over, an oil prospector visited the Tates to ask if they had ever looked for oil on their property. The family had never considered the possibility, even though ranch owners in nearby counties had struck it rich. After a couple of weeks of digging, the Tates discovered oil and in large quanti-ties. Here was a family living in poverty for years that owned, free and clear, an oil field that would eventually make the Tates multiple millions of dollars. They would have continued to live in poverty for the rest of their lives if not for an outsider who made them look in their own backyard.

As noted previously, to prospect your own acre of dia-monds (or oil field), you need to develop an external frame for your markets. Look at your business and markets as an outsider would and know your business better than anyone else and you can begin to see new opportunities.

In addition to stories of diamond mines and oil fields, sto-ries abound of companies looking in their own backyard to find considerable growth opportunities. Caterpillar Inc. is the world leader in the earthmoving equipment market, manufacturing ev-erything from tractors to diesel engines. Trying to manage a $20+ billion heavy-equipment manufacturing company would seem a logistical nightmare. But Caterpillar has effectively met the ex-treme demands of everything from inventory control to staging shipment of finished goods by developing leading-edge logistics expertise. It has become so good at logistics management that it has realized significant growth, not only from manufacturing ad-ditional earthmoving equipment, but by providing logistics ex-pertise to other companies. Caterpillar created a new division called Caterpillar Logistics Service (CLS) that provides other companies with the same expertise Caterpillar has had for years and years. CLS has grown 70 percent over the last six years. Many companies develop expertise and never see the opportunities to capitalize on it. Caterpillar took a look in its own backyard and saw a unique growth opportunity.

Similarly, the Walt Disney Company has found numerous growth opportunities by looking in its own backyard. Rather than aggressively expanding in traditional areas, such as theme parks and movie production, Disney's CEO Michael Eisner has found numerous growth opportunities that had been literally sitting right under management's noses. Shortly after Eisner arrived on the scene, he took some of Walt Disney's old videos (e.g., *Fantasia, Bambi,* and *Cinderella*) out of a vault, dusted them off, and started releasing them to the public on a limited basis; then he rereleased them a couple of years later. These videos (Disney's acres of diamonds) had been collecting dust, but Eisner was astute enough to realize their potential. The result was that Disney's video sales have contributed billions of dollars in revenues over the last couple of decades. Even the rereleasing of classics has led to significant growth; for example, the first video rerelease of *Sleeping Beauty* sold over 1 million copies.

Disney has also developed a world-class corporate culture. To socialize its new employees to the "Disney way," the corporation developed leading-edge training facilities referred to as Disney University. Another tremendous growth opportunity for the company, and management didn't even have to look outside of its backyard! Today, the Disney Institute's "Disney Approach Business and Management Program" attracts top executives from all over the world to study everything from team building to creativity. This leading-edge management development complex is situated on a 57-acre campus and uses state-of-the-art facilities (e.g., 28 learning studios). Of course, executives who use the Disney Institute facilities stay in a Disney resort and most likely take advantage of the other Disney facilities as well, resulting in significant sustainable growth for the company.

I have seen many companies trying to be all things to all people, so busy trying to find the big hit that they never stop to take a look at the potential opportunities they have around them. They never stay with a business long enough to be successful. To be a growth champion, you need to explore your own backyard. Before you go off half-cocked in search of new and exciting growth opportunities, make sure you're not overlooking the obvious. Let common sense dictate.

> We shall not cease from exploration,
> And the end of all our exploring
> Will be to find ourselves where we started
> And to know the place for the first time.
> —T. S. Elliot

Market Segmentation

Segmentation is another technique growth champions use to identify great opportunities. Segmenting markets is the process of dividing your customers into different groups based on their unique needs. Cisco Systems is growing at a rate of 1,000 new employees every month and acquires a high-tech start-up about every two weeks. Truly a remarkable growth champion, Cisco's CEO John Chambers recently stated in an interview with *The Wall Street Journal* that segmentation has allowed the company to achieve considerable growth and will continue to do so. When asked how he manages the company today differently from when he first took over, Chambers responded, "Part of the answer may surprise you. A lot of basics haven't changed. The approach we started back in '93 was one of segmenting the market." Segmentation has allowed Cisco considerable success.

Every market, regardless of customer needs, can be segmented; and growth champions are very effective at segmenting their markets—breaking a market down into its definable parts.

Different customers have different needs, and to grow your business, you must focus on customer needs and create value. Companies that try to figure out ways to take their current products and ram them down consumers' throats rather than trying to understand how value changes depending on the type of customer are destined to fail. Segmentation means opportunities and we can find numerous examples of growth champions that have entered a mature market because they saw a significant growth opportunity that current players didn't recognize.

Most would agree that the airline industry is not a growth industry. Not so—if a company is able to identify unserved segments in a mature market. Southwest Airlines has successfully served a segment of customers that demanded a no-frills airline with a great on-time track record at a low price. The result: Southwest Airlines has quickly become a growth champion by offering its services in a slow-growth market.

Another company in the same slow-growth industry has also become a growth champion by serving yet another segment of customers. Midwest Express has capitalized on an opportunity that has resulted in consistent double-digit growth over the last five years, with sales in 2000 expected to exceed $500 million. How does Midwest Express achieve such an impressive growth record in such a stagnant market? By segmenting the market, Midwest Express found a great opportunity. While clearly one segment of travelers cared only about price and convenience (paving the way for Southwest Airline's great success story), another segment of travelers wanted to be treated as first-class customers without the need to pay first-class fares. By providing numerous extras you wouldn't expect from a domestic airline, Midwest Express claims that it offers the "best care in the air." And it does. The company offers a unique combination of superior service at competitive prices. Customer service is paramount, from purchasing a ticket through baggage claims. Customers are given their choice of newspaper and a complimentary beverage prior to boarding a plane. Once on the plane, travelers enjoy extrawide leather seats, elegant meals served on china with linen napkins, and a complimentary glass of wine or champagne. The airline even bakes chocolate chip cookies—on board. Yes, Midwest Express also has a very generous frequent-flyer program; free travel starts with as little as 15,000 miles.

Serve the customer better than anyone else. By providing customers with the best possible value, Midwest Express has received numerous awards for its excellent performance. To date it has won over 15 national awards, including "Best-Managed National Airline" by *Aviation Week & Space Technology* (1998), "Best Domestic Airline" by *Travel & Leisure* (1997, 1998), and "#1 U.S. Airline" by *Conde Nast Traveler* Readers Choice Awards for the last five years in a row. In the summer of 2000, Midwest Express announced it will acquire ten additional jet aircraft to pursue additional growth opportunities.

Even if you are in a growth market, segmentation is still critical for achieving sustainable growth. In a growth market, fast growth is there for the taking, and segmentation can sustain it long after the market finishes riding the wave. Michael Dell provides an example of how segmentation works in a growth market. His contention is:

> By segmenting our business, we found the path to grow into an organization that has many different businesses. We have a business selling to large customers, to global customers, to the consumer. And these businesses have different characteristics. You separate those, and you create management opportunities. This approach not only allows us to aggressively bring talent into the company and grow talent, but also to get very finely focused on the unique needs of specialized customers and achieve high returns on invested capital.[3]

Characteristics of customer segments. To segment markets, growth champions excel at understanding characteristics of their markets. A clear recognition of the needs, concerns, and makeup of customer groups is critical because marketing, promotion, and general sales efforts are designed to appeal to and address the special concerns of each segmented group. Companies that achieve sustainable growth know firsthand that products and services are not the ends in and of themselves. In contrast, countless managers of stagnant companies often become so enamored with their products or services that they fail to understand or see customers' perspectives. Products or services, no matter how brilliantly conceived and developed, will only be successful if they provide satisfaction or meet some consumer need. Understanding the demographic and social makeup of a market segment—such as gender, age, marital status, income, occupation, and lifestyle—helps identify its needs and concerns. Whether a company is trying to appeal to a broad market or a market segment, to innovate value managers must identify specific factors that have an impact on consumers' purchasing decisions.

Sophisticated versus unsophisticated customers. During a recent consulting engagement with a fast-growth company that provides office environment management systems, I stumbled across a new way to segment markets. Most of the advice we hear about segmentation applies well to consumer markets but often leaves managers of business-to-business (B2B) markets in the dark. After struggling with segmentation issues in this context, I finally figured out a surefire way to segment customers in business-to-business markets—separate them into either a sophisticated or an unsophisticated segment. Each type of customer has a different outlook on value and each type has different "hot buttons." If you can understand what makes a customer tick, odds are you can create a growth opportunity.

- *Sophisticated customers.* Sophisticated customers understand value. They are long-term oriented and know that even if they have to pay a little more to purchase your product today, in a couple of years the quality of your product or service will pay off. Many times sophisticated customers are well informed about the product or service your company offers and may even be a long-time customer. They are sophisticated enough to know that overall value can extend well beyond the initial purchase price. For example, Caterpillar prices its products significantly higher than its competitors. How then does it remain the number one manufacturer of earthmoving equipment worldwide? Even though it sells its products at a premium price, Caterpillar offers the highest-quality products in the market and follows up with the industry's best after-sales service. In this industry, customers have to consider the initial purchase price for a piece of machinery (sometimes in the millions of dollars), but they must also consider owning and operating costs; it may cost thousands of dollars to maintain a piece of equipment each year. In addition, if a piece of equipment breaks down on the job, a customer may lose tens of thousands of dollars a day. Why are customers willing to pay a higher price for Caterpillar equipment? Caterpillar provides the best value and its customers understand value—they are sophisticated.

- *Unsophisticated customers.* In contrast, unsophisticated customers don't understand the value equation and are usually short-term oriented. They simply define value as purchase price. It may be no fault of their own if they are constrained by limited budgets or shortsighted management. And many times unsophisticated buyers are not the end users. They simply try to negotiate the best price because it is their job to save money (at least in the short run). Unsophisticated customers are usually not experienced users of the product or service. Thus, Caterpillar has considerable difficulty trying to sell equipment to unsophisticated buyers. Clearly, cheaper purchasing alternatives are available. Unsophisticated buyers may buy a cheaper piece of equipment today, thinking they just saved their company several thousand dollars. Unknown to them, however, their company will pay considerably more in maintenance costs over the next several years because unsophisticated buyers define value by purchase price.

Just because a customer may be unsophisticated doesn't mean that a significant growth opportunity is lacking. Unsophisticated customers need to be educated about value. If and when they understand value, they will become some of your most loyal customers.

Discontinuities

Discontinuities are the granddaddy of all fast-growth opportunities. Discontinuities are major shifts in a market that completely alter its condition. To the casual observer, discontinuities appear to come about suddenly, making radical alterations to a market, but discontinuities are usually the result of a cumulative set of events that progress incrementally until everything comes to a head. For example, deregulation (in banking or long-distance carriers) and technology (faxes replacing overnight document delivery and e-mail replacing faxes) have completely altered the rules of the game for many industries.

Many growth champions have the ability to define discontinuities and develop strategies to exploit these considerable growth opportunities. They focus on creating something new that can bring value to customers. They don't wait for something to happen nor imitate competition—they make things happen. They rewrite the status quo, leaving reactive companies in their wake. Some classic examples of companies that have created and/or capitalized on discontinuities are:

- Land's End, Eddie Bauer, and The Gap exploiting the acceptance of casual dress in the workplace

- Motorola's effort to liberalize mainland China's economy to create new markets for its pagers and cellular communication products

- United HealthCare's creation of HMOs to meet deregulation in the health care industry

- MCI Communication's evolution as the first competitor of AT&T as a result of deregulation

- Intel's creation and refinement of the microprocessor

In each of these examples, a company achieved incredible sustainable growth by exploiting discontinuities, and all of them have maintained double-digit growth annually for more than ten years.[4]

Businesses that successfully exploit discontinuities have the ability to see the discontinuities coming before anyone else, allowing them to seize the moment while others enviously sit on the sidelines. Identifying discontinuities is difficult, but the payoff can be tremendous. Because discontinuities can create a new industry or completely alter the competitive nature of an existing industry, growth companies are very effective in envisioning the future. Many traditional strategies rely on past information to forecast the future. Unfortunately with discontinuities, everything is new so you need to predict how a discontinuity will create opportunities and then develop strategies to exploit those opportunities.

A lot of companies have been catapulted to the top by discontinuities. Discontinuities in technology, health care, lifestyles, and the purchasing characteristics of the baby boom generation have all created significant growth opportunities. When recognized effectively, discontinuities have a significant impact on shareholder value. Companies with business models based on old assumptions put shareholder value at risk. Conversely, companies that seize opportunities created by discontinuities create significant value for shareholders. In less than one year, Netscape was able to create significant shareholder value through exploitation of discontinuities resulting from Internet technology. Gains achieved by Netscape were at the expense of IBM's "old-school" Notes GroupWare that it acquired from Lotus.

To sustain growth, sometimes growth champions create discontinuities from discontinuities. For example, Robert Noyce invented the integrated circuit. After he cofounded Intel, evolution of the 8088, 286, 386, 486, Pentium, Pentium II, and Pentium III chips created significant sustainable growth and billions of dollars in shareholder value.

Although discontinuities can take on many forms, technological advancements receive the most attention, such as Intel's average growth rate of 25 percent per year over the last 15 years. However, societal changes can also create discontinuities. For example, the increase in two-income families has created increased household wealth while simultaneously decreasing time to prepare meals for the family. Companies like Brinker International, owner of several national restaurant chains, have realized significant growth by serving this discontinuity. Discontinuities can also come from regulation and deregulation; telecommunications reform has created numerous growth opportunities for companies like MCI Communications and Sprint. Political reform can create new growth opportunities as well; the opening of China's economy has resulted in double-digit growth for Motorola.

In general, discontinuities can be separated into four major categories:

1. Technological advancements

2. Demographic shifts

3. Regulation/deregulation

4. Globalization

Technological Advancements

Obviously, technological advancements have created countless opportunities for growth. Use of the Internet and intranets has significantly affected almost every industry imaginable. Companies from Dell Computer to Wal-Mart have capitalized on changing technology. These discontinuities are forcing companies to completely restructure past practices by using Internet technology to create new business models.

As surprising as it may seem, the companies that are winning from technological advancements are not the ones focusing on technology. Why will companies that focus exclusively on technology probably lose in the new economy? Technology can be easily replicated, so growth champions focus on using technology to increase value to their customers, often through collaboration.

We hear numerous success stories of start-up companies that have evolved by serving and collaborating with some of the giant brick-and-mortar companies. Mastech was founded a decade ago by Ashok Trivedi, a product manager at Unisys, and Sunil Wadhwani, a graduate student at Carnegie Melon University. They saw a tremendous discontinuity evolving in personal computer networking. Because Mastech was an early player in local area networks, it was able to carve out a big chunk of the market. A decade ago, the company's founders were going out for a beer and to air their complaints about how large players in the network industry were still trying to force mainframes on companies that wanted network solutions for their PCs. So they created Mastech. The result: Mastech has realized tremendous growth over the last decade and today employs over 6,000 people across five continents. In the last three years the company has grown at an average annual rate of 56 percent.

Demographic Shifts

Demographic shifts refer to changing characteristics of the population. In the United States, major demographic shifts include the changing ethnicity of the population, changing family structures, and the evolution of the baby boom generation. Baby boomers have a considerable amount of wealth and have been credited with everything from the record growth of the New York Stock Exchange to the revival of the entertainment and leisure industry. Ronald Muhlenkamp, portfolio manager of the Muhlenkamp Fund, recently observed that "after building their personal balance sheets in the 1990s, baby-boom America is starting to spend for toys." Opportunities for growth are abundant for companies that have figured out ways to meet the needs of baby boomers. For example, National RV (number 24 on *Business Week*'s hot growth list) sells campers, minimotor homes, and luxury motor homes. Over the last three years, the company has had an annual average growth rate of 91 percent in earnings and sales grew at an average annual rate of 62 percent ($360 million annually). Wayne Mertes, the company's cofounder, credits the incredible growth to prosperous baby boomers wanting to spend their money on leisure activities.

Regulation/Deregulation

Regulation and deregulation can destroy or create new industries. As a discontinuity, deregulation offers considerable growth opportunities; and some individuals can even create their own discontinuity. While in medical school, Dr. Paul Ellwood was able to see the potential benefit of applying business principles to health care. In response to the rising cost of health care, Dr. Ellwood founded United HealthCare, the nation's leading HMO. The advent of HMOs quickly captured 25 percent of the health care insurance industry by 1995, and HMOs have realized significant growth by reforming a radically new approach to, yet again, a stagnant mature industry.

Over the next several years, the utility industry will become deregulated state by state. Consumers and businesses will be able to select a utility provider similarly to the way deregulation occurred in the long-distance telecommunications industry. This multitrillion-dollar discontinuity will create phenomenal growth opportunities for companies poised to exploit deregulation.

Globalization

Finally, globalization and international political reform are creating growth champions every day. As mentioned earlier, Jeff Rhodenbaugh, president and CEO of Specialty Equipment Company (number 17 in *Business Week*'s 1999 list of hot growth companies), found the U.S. market saturated. The only avenue to growth was via international expansion.

Consider the cellular phone industry. Here is an industry that has been realizing a growth rate of over 20 percent per year for the last decade. This industry started out as a business-to-business industry with Motorola taking the lead. The market quickly transitioned to general consumers ranging in age from 18 to 34. Many of these consumers wanted a cell phone that had style and flair, and Nokia took the lead by introducing various colors of cell phones that could be used as accessories. Now we see that in certain parts of the world, the age of users is getting even younger. For example, in 2000, over 25 percent of eight-year-olds surveyed in Denmark carried a cell phone. But in the cell phone industry, future growth is going to come from emerging markets. Companies are going to have to look outside the traditional U.S., European, and Japanese markets; in fact, Ericsson's fastest-growing market is mainland China.

In other product markets, Nestlé's strongest growth for its food sundries are Europe and Russia. The big three Japanese auto manufacturers have been very aggressive in developing the Southeast Asian market. The nature of the global market is changing and growth champions are quick to act on this important discontinuity.

Sources of Information: Knowing What to Look For

Why do most executives turn to published information when they want to increase their understanding of market characteristics that will have an impact on their future? General business periodicals, trade journals, government publications, and industry data are common sources and easy to obtain. The use of publications is a cornerstone of traditional views of strategic planning. Growth champions avoid the data sources everyone else uses (e.g., industry data based on four-digit SIC codes or emerging NAICS categories). Moreover, industry-level publications constrain creativity and expansion possibilities. By studying trade publications, do you think that Caterpillar would have identified logistics management as a potential growth opportunity? Would Disney have realized that executive development could lead to millions in revenues by looking at amusement park data? Clearly, the answer is no. So where are some good places to look to gain sufficient knowledge to identify great growth opportunities?

FIGURE 3.3 Sources of Information and How to Get It

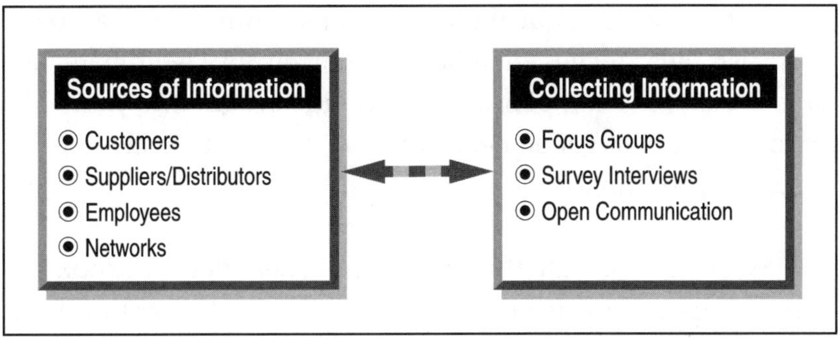

Sources of Information	Collecting Information
◉ Customers	◉ Focus Groups
◉ Suppliers/Distributors	◉ Survey Interviews
◉ Employees	◉ Open Communication
◉ Networks	

Recall that to externally frame a market, a company has to understand its customers' needs and understand its own business better than anyone else. Growth champions go directly to the source to get the information they need—customers, suppliers, employees, and competitors. Figure 3.3 shows *where* to look and *how* to look for information.

Where to Look

Customers. Customers are a tremendous source of information. One of the most innovative companies in the world, 3M, credits its long track record of developing successful new products to its ability to stay close to customers. Not only can they provide insight into what they perceive as value, but they are also useful in providing insights into how the company is doing in meeting these value perceptions.

Successful companies excel at getting a pulse on their markets by drawing ideas from customers. And they don't limit opinions to existing customers, asking potential customers for their opinions as well.

A potentially excellent source of information for understanding what's on the minds of customers is the *patterns* in customer complaints. Rather than lamenting about customer complaints, use them. They can be a great source of information for increasing your understanding of customer value. Just make sure that it's not the squeaky wheel that's getting the oil. Often a loud customer will get what he or she wants. But legitimate patterns in customer complaints may provide insight into your ability to service customers' needs or customers' misperceptions of the value you provide.

Suppliers and distributors. Companies often overlook the critical importance of involving suppliers and distributors in their data collection. Suppliers and distributors have significant input into what customers value as well as what your company can do to offer value. Quite often suppliers and distributors have valuable ideas from a different perspective. NutraSweet's Simplesse, its new fat substitute, resulted from an idea presented by a supplier. Similarly, one of Rubbermaid's newest children's lunch boxes stemmed from an idea brought up by one of its biggest retail accounts. It's often interesting to mix distributors and suppliers in focus groups where participants can feed off each other's ideas.

Employees. Talk with your employees, especially those on the front line who interact directly with customers. These employees spend every day of their working lives in the market. Overlooking this potentially rich source of information could be extremely detrimental to gaining a comprehensive understanding of value drivers.

When putting together focus groups of employees, aim for diversity. Involve employees from numerous disciplines. At a bare minimum, put salespeople, research engineers, and production managers into focus groups. Combining inputs from salespeople on the front line with the product expertise of design engineers can produce some excellent insights into value innovation.

Networks. Strategic networking—establishing relationships with important individuals or businesses outside your company—can be critical to opportunity identification. Networking relationships can take many forms and involve a variety of constituents, ranging from customer groups to trade associations to traditional competitors—yes, competitors. In the past we have been educated to never interact with competitors—they are our enemies. Numerous companies have rethought this advice and have benefited from partnering with competitors. Last month, the Big 3 U.S. auto manufacturers (GM, Ford, and DaimlerChrysler) created a multibillion-dollar network to improve supply chain management.

How to Look

Data collection can take many forms. Focus groups and surveys provide the most comprehensive base of information, but more subtle methods, such as open communication, can also provide fresh insights.

Focus groups. Focus groups are a great starting point in trying to figure out what's going on in your company and your markets. I often have my clients use focus groups as fishing expeditions to explore for fresh ideas. Focus groups provide a frame of reference to set the stage for getting more detailed information via survey interviews; reaching conclusions is not important at this stage. Remember, you're not trying to get final answers with focus groups but simply an inflow of new ideas and potential benchmarks in terms of value innovation.

The object is to bring new ideas to the surface. Although discussions may appear to be unstructured and freewheeling, a skilled researcher can unassumingly zero in on critical factors of value innovation. These sessions not only solicit important contributions from participants, but they are also an excellent vehicle for communicating a company's intent to provide outstanding value. In addition, selectively soliciting input and direction from a participant can foster understanding by and commitment from that participant, whether it's a customer, supplier or distributor, or an employee.

I encourage my clients to organize several focus groups to find out what is on the participants' minds. Focus groups should be kept fairly small (six to eight individuals) and should contain a fairly diverse set of participants. For example, if a company is trying to understand customers' issues, then bring in satisfied customers, dissatisfied customers, loyal customers, new customers, and even competitors' customers. I would be careful not to mix employees in the same focus groups as outsiders (e.g., customers, suppliers, or distributors). You'd be surprised how conservative customers' comments become when a sales representative from the company is present in a focus group session.

At this point, you may be thinking to yourself, "Sounds great, but how do we actually get people to show up?" The answer is simply a matter of framing. I have worked with clients who have been scared to ask customers to participate in focus groups. Management fears that customers will become alienated because they are already overinundated with follow-up surveys. However, I have found time and again that the way in which a company frames the *purpose* of the focus group determines how motivated participants will be. If you simply state, "Your name has been selected to be a participant in a focus group," why would someone want to show up? However, if you take the position, "We want to do whatever it takes to meet and exceed our customers' needs. We value you as a customer and your opinions. We want to know what you think—not only how satisfied you are but also what is important to you. Will you let us know what we can do to make you a more satisfied customer?" When a focus group's questions are framed well, often participants are not only willing to participate but are genuinely excited to participate. I have had clients create long-term partnerships with customers that originated in a focus group setting.

Survey interviews. Do growth companies understand the importance of collecting original data from customers via surveys? In a 1999 study of fast-growth companies conducted by Zweig White & Associates, it was found that fast-growth firms conduct surveys or original research at a rate of 33 percent more than average firms. Michael Dell believes that the "next frontier of competition is in the area of customer service and quality." So to gain access to the information that Dell feels is necessary, account teams work face-to-face with all of Dell's large customers. They also work with suppliers to stay in touch with both ends of the value chain.

Focus groups provide a basis for designing survey interviews. When structuring survey interviews, specific questions need to be formulated so they can be answered in an accurate and objective manner. I stress to clients that they need to think about the type of information they want from their survey so that questions can be structured to provide the needed answers. A survey may be designed to measure how respondents rate several purchasing drivers (e.g., price, quality, serviceability, reputation, and delivery) in terms of satisfaction and/or importance. In addition, a survey should identify demographic factors that may assist the researcher in segmenting the market (e.g., age, income level, education level, and gender). After the data are collected, the survey results may illustrate that people with a specific demographic background identify purchasing drivers that are different from those identified by people with a contrasting demographic background.

By asking respondents to rate factors based on their satisfaction and importance, a company should be able to obtain a solid foundation for understanding how it stacks up to value drivers. When interpreting survey results, I often have managers use a 2×2 matrix, plotting average responses for each survey item based on satisfaction and importance ratings as seen in Figure 3.4. A red flag to managers is when customers consistently rate an item with low satisfaction and high importance.

FIGURE 3.4 Satisfaction/Importance Matrix

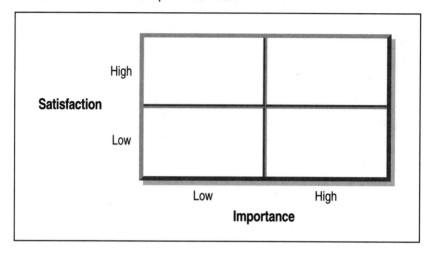

Be careful when interpreting results. I often find managers making critical decisions based on incorrect survey results. Unfortunately, they don't have much statistical knowledge and therefore make bad decisions. Having no data is better than having bad data because bad data may mislead managers and give them a false sense of security.

Make sure that the people you use in data gathering and analysis are good at what they do. A good researcher will be able to draw rich information from a group of respondents. Given the exact same situation, an inexperienced researcher will come away empty-handed or, worse yet, with incorrect findings. I have seen numerous companies try to collect their own survey information, only to end up with bad data. The reasons for bad data are numerous, ranging from poor item construction (e.g., asking leading questions) to a poor understanding of the statistical properties needed to interpret results. The best way to find a good researcher is the same as trying to find a good consultant—ask around.

Open communication. An often overlooked technique for gaining access to valuable information is plain old open communication. Many growth champions will tell you that having something as simple as an open-door policy can provide you with valuable information. Dick Blaudow, CEO of Advanced Technology Services Inc., a leading-edge industrial manufacturing service organization with an average annual growth rate of over 20 percent, contends: "I like to 'stir the pot'—to be out with my managers to talk about 'stuff' rather than staying in my office with the door shut." He accesses great information through open communication.

Growth champions also use communication to gain access to information from other stakeholders such as customers, distributors, and suppliers. For example, Ernst and Young's Entrepreneur of the Year Joe Kaplan, CEO of Innovative Merchant Solutions, says: "I like to occasionally pick up incoming telephone calls that have been routed to the customer service department. It's a great source of information for getting a pulse on what my customers are thinking." Access to information about opportunities is everywhere. For many managers it is simply a matter of opening their eyes—for the first time.

Endnotes

1. Tom Peters, "The Wow Project," *Fast Company* 24 (1999): 116–27.

2. W. Chan Kim and Renee Mauborgne, "Strategy, Value Innovation, and the Knowledge Economy," *Sloan Management Review* 40, no. 3 (1999): 41–54.

3. Michael Dell, "Maximum Speed," *Executive Excellence* 16, no. 1 (1999): 15–16.

4. Stephen H. Goldstein, "Exploit Discontinuities to Grow," *Strategies and Leadership* (September/October 1996): 12–17.

T W O

Organizational Capability Catalysts
Acquiring Skills to Drive in the Fast Lane

Recall from Chapter 1 that growth happens when preparedness crosses paths with opportunity. Now you should have a good understanding of how to identify opportunities. In the next section I address ways to prepare your company to take advantage of these opportunities.

What you won't find in this section are tools such as statistical process control mechanisms or activity based accounting systems. Specific tools vary considerably from company to company, division to division, and, moreover, they change over time. What you will find are many of the soft-skill attributes that make growth champions. I discuss the importance of creating a winning growth attitude for your organization by embracing such values as risk taking, tolerance for mistakes, curiosity, and creativity. In addition, I show how growth champions create architectures that achieve a balance between flexibility and control. Finally, I explain how to design a top management team for developing talent and maximizing growth. All of these qualities are consistent across most growth champions.

4

Redefining the Basics

Aligning a Company for Fast Growth

Numerous considerations enter into structuring a company for fast growth—ramping up operations to meet increasing demand, planning for human resources, managing costs effectively—while at the same time trying to maintain a culture that encourages creativity and embraces change. Unfortunately, many companies get so caught up in the concept of core competencies that they never have a chance to design a winning organization.

We hear much about developing core competencies, which seems to be the central focus for many companies. When I ask most managers in executive development seminars for their company's core competencies, they rattle off a couple of factors without missing a beat. Often these competencies have been passed down from preceding generations of managers, and current executives accept them as givens.

I don't care about core competencies and neither do growth champions. Whenever I tell a group that core competencies should not be a company's central focus, I receive interesting looks—some perplexed, others curious. But the most common look is one of skepticism. "What do you mean don't focus on core competencies?" they ask. "That's how we identify opportunities. It's what our company is all about—it's our lifeblood, our future!" they claim defensively.

Core competencies are internally focused. They represent factors that management feels are critical to the business—but critical based usually on management's opinion. Most companies believe the best way to grow is to try to understand their sources of core competencies and figure out ways to exploit them.

Now consider that growth champions maintain a steady revenue stream yet manage traditional core competencies very differently than most ordinary companies. Growth champions allow core competencies to evaporate. Growth champions don't commit to a specific core competence. Core competencies are fluid, coming and going depending on changing value drivers in a particular market. Rather than focusing on core competencies and then looking for opportunities to exploit them, growth champions figure out how to build or acquire skills and capabilities necessary to innovate value for a market's changing needs.

Challenging Traditional Thinking

I have already asked you to reconsider several central themes of traditional strategic thinking. Almost every company that goes through the strategic-planning process uses some sort of strengths, weaknesses, opportunities, and threats (SWOT) analysis. Over the years, SWOT analysis has probably done more harm than good, but used correctly, it can provide valuable insights into organizations. Unfortunately, most companies take the SWOT model too literally.

Because the acronym is SWOT, they begin the planning process by identifying sources of strengths and weaknesses with an internally generated perspective. But how can a company identify its strengths and weaknesses if it doesn't have a good understanding of its markets? Moreover, based on *current* strengths and weaknesses (probably generated by upper-level management in a half-day retreat), it proceeds to identify opportunities and threats. In other words, it lets its internal strengths and weaknesses define its markets.

Most companies consider growth opportunities as alternative ways to exploit their resources and capabilities. Their approach to exploitation of opportunities: "Given that we have a certain combination of resources and capabilities to attempt to create a sustainable competitive advantage, what options are available to us?" They limit themselves by what they currently have, looking only at their competencies to pursue new growth opportunities. This is backward thinking.

In contrast, growth champions don't ask what they can do with what they currently have. They ask how, given potential changes in the market, will they have to change their combination of resources and skills to align with these new demands. Rather than focusing on core competencies, growth champions try to develop *distinctive competencies.* The basic difference between these concepts is that core competencies are based on what a company does well (based on the company's own opinion), whereas distinctive competencies are based on what a company does well *relative to its market's value drivers.*

Only after they have a solid understanding of the value drivers in their markets do growth champions even consider a critical assessment of their resources and capabilities to develop distinctive competencies. Rather than letting capabilities drive growth opportunities (the core competence approach), successful companies let growth opportunities drive sources of distinctive competencies. Stated differently, core competencies are internally benchmarked—based on management's opinion—whereas distinctive competencies are externally benchmarked—based on value drivers.

If growth companies don't have the assets and skills necessary to meet a growth opportunity, they figure out ways to get them, whether internally, through a strategic alliance, or externally, through an acquisition. The British music company Virgin Group asked itself how it could start all over again to grow. In the late 1980s the company had a large chain of traditional music stores. Remember (from the last chapter) Richard Branson, Virgin's chairman and president—the one who writes down everything he observes, accumulating literally hundreds of notebooks of ideas? Well, one of those ideas paid off in a huge way. Noticing that the megastore concept was creating value in other industries, the Virgin Group believed it would work in its industry too. Knowing that its current chain of small stores couldn't be leveraged to innovate value using a megastore approach, the company started all over. It sold off the company's chain of stores, which allowed the company to innovate value by offering megastores specializing in music and entertainment. This resulted in a huge growth for Virgin and reshaped an old industry in the UK by discovering a better way to offer value to customers. One of Virgin's senior executives summed it all up by saying, "We don't let what we can do today condition our view of what it takes to win tomorrow. We take a clean slate approach."[1]

Growth champions also realize, as noted, that sources of distinctive competencies come and go; they are not ends in themselves because rivals can trump sources of competitive advantage. To always stay ahead of the pack, a company has to be adaptable so it can continually develop new sources of distinctive competencies to meet changing market needs. Often, companies that have achieved past success are slow to realize their source of competitive advantage is eroding. They bury their heads in the sand, hoping that competitors will go away. This is when rivals overtake them. To avoid this, companies have to understand how their combination of resources and capabilities influences customers to purchase products from them and not someone else.

As we have already seen, to achieve sustainable growth and long-term value, managers must cultivate the right frames and attitudes among employees at all levels. Management needs to anticipate shocks. Every resource a company has is vulnerable. Growth champions are superb at:

- Identifying the resources their companies need to be successful in the future

- Taking action to start building those resources

For taking actions to build resources, however, most companies immediately think of accumulating tangible resources (e.g., buying a better plant or better equipment). In contrast, growth companies know the resources that lead to sustainable growth are intangible soft-skill resources such as creativity, culture, expertise, and innovation. Although most competencies are relatively short-lived, soft-skill resources are the types of competencies that keep a growth champion thriving—and it all starts with attitude.

Creating a Growth Attitude

Your attitude shapes your environment. Successful companies don't develop good attitudes; good attitudes develop successful companies. When working with clients, I often discuss initiatives that lead to growth, and the conversation quickly turns to technology. Technology is fast-paced, exciting, and often provocative. But a company develops and exploits new technology by having the right combination of soft skills (e.g., curiosity, expertise, and support). To create a successful company in any business, you must have an effective culture.

To create a growth champion, you must create an attitude for growth—a culture that fosters creativity, encourages risk taking, and is accepting of mistakes.

Growth champions do the basics very well. For some of them, depending on their industry, doing the basics well is all it takes to create a growth champion.

Culture can dramatically influence top-line growth and bottom-line profits, and a change in culture can reignite employees. According to *Fortune* magazine, Emerson Electric's CEO Chuck Knight has injected new life into the 110-year-old company by radically altering its corporate culture. To instill a growth culture, Knight centers his initiatives on an annual two-day growth conference conducted by each of the organization's divisions. Division presidents take this very seriously, often spending several months preparing for the conference. Why do they make such significant efforts for the conference? Knight is dedicated to growth and he expects nothing less of his people. In addition, employees' pay is tied to meeting growth objectives.

In the last five years, sales of Emerson Electric have grown from $8.6 billion to $14.3 billion. Moreover, in 1999, Emerson celebrated its 42nd consecutive year of increased earnings and increased earnings per share. Why radically shift direction when a company has had so much past success? Because shifting direction is what makes a growth champion remain a growth champion. For years, Emerson aggressively squeezed costs. As noted in Chapter 1, long-term, bottom-line profits from growth will increase shareholder value; bottom-line profits from cost cutting won't.

So Chuck Knight decided to shake things up. According to Knight, reinventing the company is part of his standard operating procedure. The company even has "change the game" initiatives each year whose goal is to drive customer and shareholder value.

Growth champions are constantly working on their cultures—an ongoing process. This doesn't mean that they are constantly trying to change their overall culture, but it does mean they are constantly trying to improve their culture. The result? Breakthroughs in defining new products, figuring out better

FIGURE 4.1   The Nine Keys to a Winning Growth Attitude

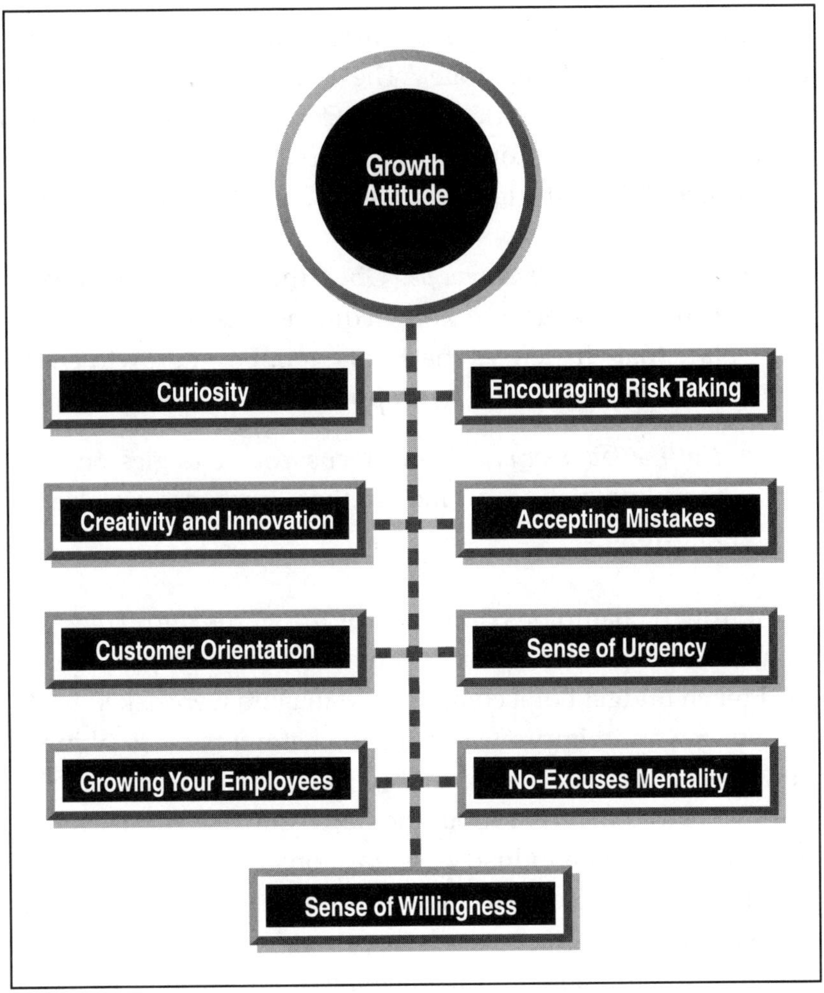

ways to deliver service, developing new business models to increase speed, and increasing ways to simplify customers' purchasing experiences—the result of the right attitude. To create and manage a growth attitude that fosters creativity and breakthroughs, I have observed nine key attributes that growth champions use, as seen in Figure 4.1. Different companies place a different emphasis on each of these components, yet each is present in most growth champions' cultures.

Curiosity: Challenging the Status Quo

I hear all too often, "We do things this way because this is the way it's always been done." The "if it's not broken, don't fix it" mentality doesn't work anymore. Companies that follow this approach will become tomorrow's losers. Henry David Thoreau once stated: "Obey the law that reveals, not the law revealed."

- *Obey the law that reveals.* Obey the law that unveils or exposes underlying knowledge not visible to most, the law that challenges the status quo. For a growth champion, this may mean new opportunities to provide value.

- *Not the law revealed.* Don't focus your energies on common knowledge, on factors that everyone else already knows.

Growth champions don't accept the status quo. They constantly challenge assumptions. Remember the example of Accor, the French budget hotel company? Managers were asked to figure out a way to improve service to customers by thinking of new ways to provide a good night's sleep at an affordable price. They were told to forget about the status quo and think in terms of value rather than industry assumptions.

It can be hard to realize that procedures that made sense in the past are now unnecessarily constraining or restricting. For example, a requirement of management approval for expenditures can help ensure cost containment and build a culture of careful attention to financial control. Yet this same approach can slow decision making and frustrate managers as a business grows.

Unfortunately, procedures and routines breed a life of their own. Often, we stick with them simply because "that's the way we've always done it."

> Growth companies challenge existing routines, con-
> stantly questioning if there is a better way to do
> things. "Good enough" doesn't cut it anymore.

Foster Creativity and Innovation

GE has killed the NIH (not invented here) culture. CEO Jack Welch says that by decimating bureaucracy, GE's culture has opened itself up to new ideas from everyone everywhere. Open-minded behavior has become a natural part of GE's culture.

We often think of innovation as an exciting way to create a new growth champion. However, a resurgence of innovation can also teach an old dog new tricks. In the mid-1990s, Hewlett-Packard's oldest business unit—the test and measurement business—was on its way out the door. Rather than the group rolling over and dying, Ned Barnholt, the group's general manager, says the group rededicated itself to innovation, which meant going far beyond product innovation. The business had to reinnovate its strategy, its culture, and every other aspect of its business. According to Barnholt, "We looked for innovative ways to change our processes, our organization, our culture—and our products—so that we could not only survive in a fast-paced environment, but grow."

Focus on Customers

As discussed in the last chapter, it is critical to keep communication lines with customers open. Jack Welch credits much of GE's success to a change in orientation from a provider of products augmented by services to a customer-focused company that provides high-value information and technology-based solutions.

Recall that one of the best ways to stay ahead of the pack is to stay in close contact with customers and those you would like to have as customers. If managers pay careful attention, customers will often signal changes, improvements, and innovations that are needed. Further, customers will also signal areas of growth where meaningful business opportunities may exist. Having a focus on customers is much more than relying on secondary published data. Market research databases are not a substitute for close relationships with customers.[2]

Growing Your Employees

There may be no better engine for a solid growth attitude than investing in employees. Given limited resources, many average companies invest only in short-term bottom-line activities. Buying a new machine or purchasing a new software program takes precedence over funds committed to the training and development of people. Training exposes people to new ideas, new ways of thinking, and new options for the business. Many times, training is fertile ground for the development of ideas and innovations that help the business position itself for growth. Jere Stead, former chairman of Square D and Legent Corporation, once said that if he had $1 to spend, he would spend it on training. From training comes the insight needed to survive and grow.

Making Willingness the Rule

Many companies motivate their employees to get a job done by coercion. "If you don't get the job done, you're fired!" The use of threats is not going to promote employee willingness to go the extra mile. And that's exactly the type of employee you're going to need to develop if you want to become a growth champion. To begin to promote an attitude of willingness, the company needs to support employees with sufficient resources and knowledge. Knowledge is the most critical resource in innovating value. You can't force the development of knowledge, but you can provide the right environment to encourage the development of knowledge.

Encouraging Risk Taking

Managers of growth companies encourage their people to be active risk takers. Fast-growth companies like 3M reward successful risk takers more aggressively than do average companies. Average companies reward employees for managing their budgets and cutting costs rather than for breakthrough ideas. Recognize what this statement says, and, even more important, recognize what it does not say. Risk taking does not represent wild, off-the-cuff whimsical movements that have a gut-level feel that they make sense and will prove to be business winners. Risk taking is careful and deliberate. It requires study and examination. Yet it recognizes there are no certainties in growing markets. At some point, the business must step forward and make its best, well-calculated decision, even though that decision may entail uncertainty and risk.

Growth companies provide support so that employees can develop an intimate knowledge of the business, customer needs, and value drivers. They encourage employees to think beyond traditional answers and take calculated risks. And they create an environment that protects young, promising businesses from old, floundering businesses. For example, Hewlett-Packard makes a considerable effort to avoid the "drowning-man syndrome." An old business trying to grow can be like a drowning person, pulling all of the resources to itself and ultimately drowning itself and potential new businesses. So H-P separates its old and new businesses, allowing each type to pursue its own risks.

Be Accepting of Mistakes

Any company that aggressively pursues growth will make mistakes, but growth champions are able to quickly learn from their mistakes and move forward, repairing problems on the run. Michael Dell says that his company is truly proud of having made mistakes and learned from them. To him, the answer is not in having perfectly developed the most prosperous ideas before you start a new business. Rather, it is the ability to learn from your mistakes so that you don't repeat them and making sure these lessons are passed along as the organization evolves and grows.

Many managers pay lip service to *risk taking*, a popular buzzword in a lot of companies. Unfortunately, many of these same managers, through their own failed risks, actually discourage risk taking because they are intolerant of mistakes. Growth champions realize that, by nature, taking risks often results in mishaps and mistakes. Sometimes, even the most thought-out and carefully planned strategies end in failure. Reasons for failure are numerous—a market may suddenly change or the economy takes an unexpected dip. When a risky venture fails, growth companies jump right back on their bikes and start peddling. Mistakes are a necessary evil of risk taking, but risk taking leads to growth opportunities.

Innovative managers understand mistakes. They view mistakes as natural outcomes of creativity. They dissect mistakes, trying to find out when, where, and how things went wrong. Mistakes are learning opportunities that can be used to avoid future mistakes.

A classic example illustrates this point. Many years ago, a young manager was called to the office of IBM founder Tom Watson. The young manager had misread a risky venture. Though he had carefully studied and prepared, the strategies he proposed failed in the uncertain and dynamic information technology environment. Although he could have played it safe, but the manager took a calculated risk that cost the company more than $10 million. Sitting in Watson's office, the young manager fidgeted nervously and offered his resignation. Watson's response was quick and decisive. "You can't be serious. We've just spent $10 million educating you." Watson's message and its impact are clear. Mistakes are part of continuous learning in a creative environment.

Have a Sense of Urgency

The rules have changed. Businesses have to react to opportunities with lightning speed. New products are getting from the drawing table to market three to four times faster than they did a few years ago. This need for speed has created a sense of urgency in many companies. Speed in and of itself is now a critical capability needed for success in many industries. New business models are evolving in e-time, using the Internet to make speed one of the newest competitive weapons in any successful company's arsenal. In addition to using technology to create speed, growth companies create a sense of urgency in their culture. Outstanding responsiveness to customer needs is a strength of many growth champions. Growth companies create environments to allow employees to be able to maintain this high level of responsiveness by empowering employees on the front line to provide total solutions for customers. This same sense of urgency encourages employees to think beyond customers' current needs, often filtering into areas such as product and process development. This often means letting products cannibalize each other. Microsoft, Intel, and Lucent Technologies accept the fact that their new products often cannibalize existing products.

No-Excuses Mentality

Earlier in the book, I talked about how managers of average companies are masters at developing excuses for why they cannot grow their business. Surprisingly, most companies encour-

FIGURE 4.2   The Three Rs of Maintaining Culture

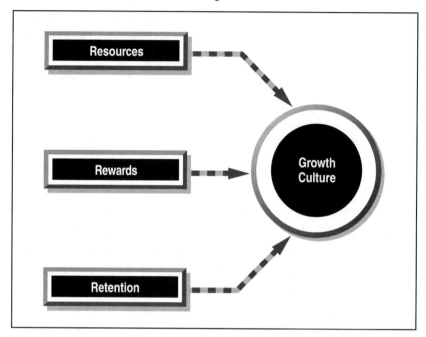

age this behavior simply by letting their employees get away with it. Growth champions are not tolerant of excuses. Their attitude is, "If you hit a stumbling block, step back and figure out another way to get the job done." Expectancy is a key part of their culture.

*G*rowth companies expect to succeed.

Companies that don't expect to succeed won't succeed. If a company with a no-excuses mentality hits a wall, it views it as a minor setback and then figures out another way to move forward. Great growth companies are able to continually move ahead rather than coming up with excuses. They are willing to re-create the rules of the game if that's what it takes to grow.

The Three Rs of Maintaining Culture

It is critical to develop the right culture for growth. Certain individual characteristics of the culture may change, but it is important to support and maintain the overall culture once it has been established. In addition to the nine factors critical in developing a winning growth attitude, I have also noticed three critical activities (as shown in Figure 4.2) that can help to sustain an effective culture: (1) providing resources to promote the values that a culture dictates; (2) providing a reward system for employees who behave in ways that support the culture; and (3) retaining the culture by socializing new employees to the values of the organization.

Resources

Companies often spend years trying to develop a new culture, an attitude for growth, only to see it slowly wither and dry up. How do growth champions maintain a fast-paced growth culture over a long period of time? One action they perform to maintain culture is to provide the resources necessary for employees to support the company's values.

Outback Steakhouse has realized very significant growth in North America and Asia. In a market most would consider stagnant, Outback has grown to over 450 restaurants and annual revenues of over a billion dollars in less than ten years. Outback management attributes its success to the company's ability to provide sufficient resources (e.g., facilities and training) to its employees (at every level) to support the company's strong culture. At Outback, the company's most critical value is quality.

Some of you may be wondering if quality is a cultural value. Yes, quality as conceived by W. Edward Demming, the father of total quality management (TQM), is a cultural value; it is not about quality circles, defect rates, or statistical process control models. Quality is an internal value that should be ingrained in everyone from the CEO to the receptionist at the front door. Outback Steakhouse understands this, and it is a central part of its culture. How does Outback provide resources to support its culture? First, it has enlarged its kitchens, making them much bigger than industry standards, because Outback thought it was important to provide employees with an environment that allowed them to maintain and improve the quality of food preparation.

Another effort Outback made to provide the right environment for its employees to deliver on quality was the actual layout of its restaurants. Waiters and waitresses serve only half as many tables as a typical restaurant, which allows them to provide outstanding customer service. Employees report they get bigger tips because of their quality service, and the quality service makes a stressful job more fun. The bottom line is that quality is central to Outback's culture, and to maintain that culture, Outback makes calculated efforts to provide an environment and resources that allow employees to support the culture.

Rewards

In a recent survey of growth companies by Sibson & Company, an international management consulting firm, it was found that high-growth companies' reward systems were sufficiently different from those at most companies. Over 80 percent of growth companies set their executives' salaries at a competitive average and the other 20 percent set them below the market average. However, executives' incentive compensation opportunities at growth companies were above average, resulting in total payout opportunities that were above average. Conversely, low-growth companies rewarded executives with above-average salaries but smaller incentive compensation opportunities.[3] Through the use of reward systems, growth companies instill the idea of risk taking.

Fast-growth companies create programs that aggressively identify key actions that lead to growth. In the Sibson study, 90 percent of growth companies had an explicit measure of growth (e.g., revenues/sales volume) in executives' compensation programs. Only 22 percent of average performers did the same. Some fast-growth companies even used growth kickers. One of the CEOs in Sibson's study told his executive team that the entire team would be given a large one-time reward if it grew 15 percent per year over the next three years. Another interesting finding from this study showed that only 40 percent of fast-growth companies use return on investment (ROI) as a key performance indicator. And of the minority of companies that do use ROI, it was usually in combination with some other growth-based measures. Conversely, 67 percent of average performers used ROI and cash flow measures without any accompanying growth measures.

At Cisco Systems, a central value to its culture is customer satisfaction. To stress the importance of this central value, Cisco ties performance to its values. John Chambers, Cisco's CEO, states, "Then we pay every manager on customer satisfaction. It's amazing how that works. Once you say it's going to be part of their compensation, people say this must really be important."

Retention

As a company grows rapidly, new employees are often hired at a tremendous rate. For the last two years, Nokia has increased its number of employees at a rate of 210 percent per year. The challenge: integrating new employees with existing employees and trying to maintain a consistent culture with the huge influx of new blood. Adding large numbers of new employees is exciting. Different people with different backgrounds and experience are bound to bring new ideas into the company's mainstream communication channels; however, managers must ensure that the company doesn't lose its identity. New employees are often thrown into the front line so quickly that they don't have a chance to understand the values the company is based on. As they become managers of other new employees, the cycle continues until the company eventually loses its identity.

What does this mean? As a company brings in new employees, it must take time to socialize them into the company's culture, even though this may be difficult during periods of high growth. Find the time—it's worth the effort. Socialization could be in the form of training and mentoring. Short term–oriented companies don't feel they have the time to show new employees the ropes during a period of high growth; and short term–oriented companies are usually failures in the long run. Conversely, long term–oriented companies ensure that new employees are indoctrinated into the culture, even if it means a little extra effort for both the company and the new employees.

The Flexibility/Control Paradox: Creating the Right Organizational Architecture for Growth

There is a paradox involving flexibility and control. Many firms strive for flexibility because flexible organizational structures encourage creativity. Other firms strive for increased control because control leads to effective cost management. Unfortunately, the more flexible an organization tries to be, the less control it has, resulting in poor cost management. Conversely, as a company becomes more control oriented, it loses flexibility, as seen in Figure 4.3.

Ideally, successful businesses would like to have the flexibility of an entrepreneurial company and the cost control of a well-established multinational. Growth companies achieve balance between these two extremes. They figure out ways to allow their companies to pursue growth opportunities and still manage costs. Usually, growth champions find ways to integrate

FIGURE 4.3   The Flexibility/Control Paradox

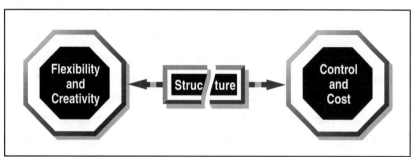

strategic objectives, culture, and capabilities to allow for both flexibility and control.

Flexibility: Creativity through Agility

It's critical to keep a company agile and flexible in the face of changes in its environment. Growth champions are not lulled by complacency and layers of bureaucracy. According to Jack Welch, a growth company "breathes information, loves change and is excited about the opportunity that change presents." To encourage flexibility, Welch has the most appropriate people solve problems — regardless of where they are in the organizational hierarchy — because Welch "hates bureaucracy and all the nonsense that goes with it." Flexibility is paramount to GE, and Jack Welch makes a concerted effort to see it stays that way.

There are numerous ways to achieve flexibility. A textbook explanation of how to achieve a flexible organization would include empowering employees to make decisions and creating a flat organizational structure. There are, however, countless other ways (some of them very subtle) by which a growth champion achieves flexibility — most of them not found in textbooks.

For example, Hewlett-Packard's secret to maintaining flexibility is its Management by Wandering Around (MBWA) program. MBWA is an informal H-P practice that involves keeping up-to-date with individuals and activities through informal or unstructured communication. Trust and respect for individuals are apparent when MBWA is used to recognize employees' concerns and ideas. MBWA is accomplished in a variety of ways. Some managers consistently reserve time to walk through their department or be available for impromptu discussions. It may also involve individual networking across the organization, coffee talks, communication lunches, and hallway conversations.

Efforts at encouraging open communication are also critical to designing flexibility into Cisco Systems' organizational architecture. John Chambers makes a concerted effort to stay in touch with his employees through a variety of approaches. One approach he uses is his Birthday Breakfast program; once a month anybody who had a birthday during that month can have a sit-down breakfast with Chambers to ask questions. "Anything is fair game" attests Chambers. Directors and VPs are not allowed to attend because Chambers interacts with them on a daily or weekly basis. Birthday breakfasts are a chance for Chambers to meet with employees he usually doesn't get a chance to interact with. Chambers sincerely believes he benefits from these meetings as well as the employees: "And every single time I learn two or three things that either I need to do differently, or things I thought were working one way weren't."

Most of the time managers try to streamline their operations, eliminating redundant or repetitious tasks to make them more efficient. However, in some situations redundancy can be a good thing by encouraging flexibility. Why would a company encourage two employees to do the same task at the same time? Innovative "poster child" 3M intentionally builds redundancy into its systems by providing employees a certain percentage of free time to "dream dreams." Managers at 3M credit this potential redundancy as their key to remaining at the leading edge of technology development. Companies that overburden themselves with cost-cutting initiatives would see this as simply a waste of time and resources and a good opportunity to trim some excess fat. Some companies have become so "anorexic" that they don't have the flexibility to seize new growth opportunities.[4] For companies in highly dynamic markets that must be able to react quickly to change, potential redundancies via experimentation are acceptable because they are part of the company's recipe for flexibility.

A word of caution: flat organizational structures are not always the elixir for encouraging creativity that many managers assume them to be. A major downside to a flat structure is that upper-level management will have a huge span of control. If a company has a flat structure, it must delegate decision-making responsibility to lower-level employees. Otherwise, the same flat organizational structure the company designed to encourage flexibility and creativity will actually destroy innovation. If the CEO has 10 to 20 people reporting to him or her, a decision-making bottleneck occurs. The CEO will be so overinundated with putting out day-to-day fires that he or she will never have time to step back and see the big picture—one of the most important functions of a CEO in a growth company.

Control: Chasing Your Tail to Ramp Up Operations

One of the biggest control challenges that growth champions are able to overcome is the ability to build an organization that can match the opportunity. Have you ever watched a dog try to catch its tail? It will run around in circles for hours on end. The harder it tries to catch its tail, the faster it goes, yet it will never catch up with its tail. Many businesses play the same game. The faster they grow, the harder they try to keep up with demand. The harder they try, the further they fall behind.

The difficulty many fast-growth firms face is trying to use structures and business models that aren't built to handle growth. They lose control and can't keep up with the growth they have worked so hard to achieve. Managers start to curse growth rather than embrace it. Eventually, operations hit a wall and the firm's infrastructure comes crashing down. Unfortunately, it's not as simple as adding a few new employees with every new major account you land. Often, the company's organizational architecture has to be redesigned for the company to control its growth.

Growth champions are able to sustain and benefit from growth because they have the control systems in place before growth occurs. As a company grows in size, certain procedures need to become standardized. Approaches to serving customers must be consistent. The Chicago-based information technology (IT) consulting firm Whitman Hart has undergone a growth restructuring. For almost a decade the company has grown at an average annual rate of 40 percent. Senior partner Stan Martin confesses that "growth companies tend to lack foresight. We didn't want to be like that as we got bigger." So in 1997, Whitman decided to standardize the way the company markets, services customers, and communicates internally. Martin continues: "We need to ensure that there are formal procedures in place. That's the only way we can continue to grow."

Breaking Out of a Cost-Cutting Mentality

Another control issue related to growth is effective cost management. Most companies fail to realize the huge difference between effective cost management and cost cutting. Effective cost management focuses on the best allocation of a limited amount of funds to maximize performance. Investing capital in the development of new resources and capabilities is a zero-sum situation. Investing in one opportunity takes money away from another potential opportunity. Because resources are limited, managers of growth companies are very good at assessing risk in deciding where to spend their money. Numerous metrics exist to measure the success of invested dollars. At Dell, management found itself reprioritizing and refocusing its growth opportunities by using ROI to measure different parts of its business. "If the cost of capital is 15 percent and a business is earning 20 percent return on invested capital, it's creating value for our shareholders" says Michael Dell. "When we sorted through our businesses, we had some businesses with very high ROI and very low growth, and we had some businesses with very low ROI and very high growth. We didn't want either of those. We wanted reasonable ROI and reasonable growth."

However, many businesses focus only on cost-cutting attributes to improve return measures, and this mentality becomes ingrained in management. Making cost cutting the focal point of an organization is a sure way to kill growth. In a recent interview with *Fortune* magazine, Emerson Electric's CEO Chuck Knight confesses that "we got so bottom line–oriented that we were inhibiting growth. We were cutting, cutting. But you can only go so far." Businesses that have been seriously pursuing cost-cutting strategies in areas like inventory management, improved operational efficiencies, and the like can quickly lose their focus on effectively utilizing resources to maximize performance. Knight continues:

> It's just been amazing to be sitting in these conferences, looking at these growth programs, and thinking "Why the hell haven't we done some of this stuff before?" Well, we hadn't done it because we didn't have the resources to do it. And we didn't have the resources to do it because we were pounding the shit out of profit margins.[5]

Pursuit of growth doesn't mean you forget about controlling costs. What it does mean is that a company makes a determined commitment to growth through its allocation of resources.

It seems that companies go through endless cycles of cost cutting punctuated by periods of growth. Consider a scenario where there are five companies in a market with each trying to achieve 25 percent market share, adding up to 125 percent — a major competitive concern. Obviously, most companies in the industry fail to meet projections. The reaction: everyone scales back and focuses on cost cutting. Weaker players get squeezed out of the market. Now let's say there are only three firms left, each conservatively expecting to achieve 20 percent of the market, which adds up to only 60 percent. Suddenly these companies find it easy to grow again. New players are attracted to the market and the whole cycle starts all over again.

To break this cycle and create an effective cost-management program (as opposed to cutting costs), having an attitude that we can always do better and good isn't good enough is an essential ingredient. General Motors used this very attitude to develop an innovative cost-management model. The company's international development of its standardized plant was radically different from anything that had been done in the past. The company created regional hubs in Argentina, Poland, Thailand, and China, each incorporating its own supplier networking system for each specific part of the world. Standardizing its plants worldwide created significant economies of scale to improve overall cost management. Regional hubs further improved cost management by allowing each hub to create a supplier network to meet the unique demands for that particular region, resulting in improved efficiencies and flexibility.

Achieving Balance: The Natural Order of Structure

There are obviously benefits to being flexible and benefits to having control. Both are needed for a company to manage growth. How can a growth company achieve a balance between flexibility and control? Michael Dell suggests, "Structure should come last, not first."

Figure 4.4 illustrates the order in which structure evolves. First, a company must understand the underlying drivers that

FIGURE 4.4   The Natural Order of Structure

innovate value. After managers have a fundamental understanding of value drivers, they can develop strategies to exploit those drivers, such as making sure the company has the resources to meet its growth objectives and a plan to fulfill customers' needs. After the strategy is in place, then the company needs to develop a structure to meet the plan. Therefore, if a company defines itself by its structure, it will severely limit its exploitation of growth opportunities. Instead, as value drivers change, strategies and structure will change.

As a company experiences growth, past job descriptions will likely become obsolete. As Dell Computer has grown, management has divided and subdivided jobs. At first, says Michael Dell, people complain that their job is being cut in half. As the company grows, it quickly becomes a full-time job again. Soon employees are begging for their job to be cut in half again.

Netscape provides an example of a growth champion that has learned, through trial and error, how to effectively maintain the flexibility of a small start-up while still acting like a multi-billion-dollar company. Its approach was to continually decentralize, breaking the structure into many small teams. Netscape's intent in committing to a team approach was to have large-company cost-control systems and still maintain flexibility and creativity through the creation of numerous small teams.

Almost every company begins with a simple structure based on functional groups (e.g., marketing, finance, and production). Netscape was no different. As the company began to grow in size, product divisions replaced functional groups. Flexibility was critical to Netscape as the industry evolved. Speed was paramount as the company tried to stay at the leading edge of Internet technology. Teaming provided the only legitimate platform to keep the flexibility needed for speed while maintaining the ability to coordinate and control a big business. Small autonomous teams allow focus on a common business rather than functional-level constraints inherent in most organizations. Giving a sufficient amount of freedom to the team is critical. Empowerment increases a feeling of ownership. The more employees take ownership, the more pride they take in completing their tasks.

Hewlett-Packard has also been very successful at balancing flexibility and control. To achieve this balance, H-P believes the most critical component is open communication, which is at the core of its culture. Management believes that given the right tools, training, and information for doing a good job, people will contribute their best. H-P has shown that open communication leads to three fundamental benefits:

1. Strong teamwork between employees, customers, and others

2. Enhanced achievement and contribution

3. Customer relationships built on trust and respect

Although most companies never get past the flexibility/control paradox, growth champions are able to figure out ways to have the best of both worlds. Most of the time it is not based on leading-edge technological advancements reserved for the most brilliant companies. Instead, growth champions often go back to the basics to achieve the proper balance between flexibility and control:

- Improved speed in problem solving via team building

- Simplification of formal control systems

- Increased frequency of face-to-face contact among managers

- Empowering employees to take ownership and rewarding them accordingly

- Encouraging open communication throughout the organization

Endnotes

1. W. Chan Kim and Renee Mauborgne, "Value Innovation: The Strategic Logic of High Growth," *Harvard Business Review* (January-February 1997): 103–12.

2. Sam Hill and Glenn Rifkin, *Radical Marketing* (New York, NY: Harper Business, 1999).

3. Jude T. Rich, "The Growth Imperative," *Journal of Business Strategy* 20, no. 2 (1999): 27–31.

4. Alan Mitchell, "Corporate Dieting Can Make Your Company Fat," *Management Today* (May 1998): 42–48.

5. Ronald Henkoff, "Growing Your Company: Five Ways to Do It Right!" *Fortune* (November 25, 1996): 78–85.

Walking the Talk

Leading a Growth Champion

As this book attests, successful growth can be attributed to effective leadership. Leaders guide their companies on how to see markets. They create and determine the underlying values and philosophies who define a winning culture. They are responsible for the development and deployment of strategies that will keep the company profitable. Leaders are responsible for positioning their companies for growth. Whether you lead an entire corporation or a group within a corporation, effective leadership of your employees is critical—every step of the way—in trying to become a growth champion.

Because every topic in this book is related to or impacted by leadership, an entire chapter is devoted to leadership because leadership is a key ingredient in sustaining growth. A company can create short-term growth in numerous ways but effective leadership sustains growth. A lot of information on leadership has appeared over the past several years—seminars, books, and magazine articles advising would-be leaders about change management, visioning, coaching, empowerment, and charismatic and transformational leadership. All of this advice is important in becoming an effective leader. But it doesn't help in distinguishing growth champions from ordinary companies. Admittedly, leaders of growth champions have many, if not all, of the qualities considered necessary for leadership, but so do many leaders of failing companies. So rather than rehashing a lot of mainstream leadership advice you could pick up from a popular book on leadership, this chapter explores leadership issues that are unique to fast-growth companies.

What makes an effective leader of a growth company? What unique challenges does the leader of a growth business have to face? How do leaders of growth businesses push leadership down to lower levels of management to create *growth domains* within their organization? Even more basic, whom do we consider the leaders of growth businesses? There are four major themes integrated through this chapter that any manager of a growth business has to master:

1. Playing the dual role of an entrepreneurial opportunist and a pragmatic realist

2. Building a winning top management team by recruiting top talent and designing a diverse team

3. Creating growth domains within the organization by pushing leadership down to all levels through effective communication

4. Organizing human resources to manage growth in a fast-paced setting by delegating talent development and mentoring

Playing the Dual Role of Opportunist and Realist: Dreamers and Doers

Leaders of growth companies have unique qualities, many of which, fortunately, can be learned. Leaders of growth companies are excellent at aggressively envisioning—stepping back and continually exploring—the big picture for new opportunities.

> *L*eaders of growth champions don't sit back to enjoy their previous success—they relentlessly pursue growth.

They use success (and failure) as a classroom, learning from each previous experience how to identify new opportunities. Companies that sit back and enjoy today's success become tomorrow's failures. However, it is not enough to simply identify growth opportunities. Leaders of growth companies must also initiate and maintain action to exploit these opportunities. Remember, growth occurs when preparedness meets opportunity.

To habitually identify and exploit growth opportunities, leaders of growth champions achieve balance by playing a dual role as seen in Figure 5.1. On one hand, they must be opportunists, trying to identify growth opportunities that others don't see — that is, they must be entrepreneurial. In this role, leaders of growth companies must have the ability to step back to see the big picture. They must be able to anticipate needs and innovate value. Part of being an opportunist means that leaders of growth companies are willing to stick their necks out, to take risks. Sometimes these risks pay off big. Other times, the risks may not pay off at all, and leaders of growth champions are aware of this.

FIGURE 5.1   The Dual Role of Growth Leaders

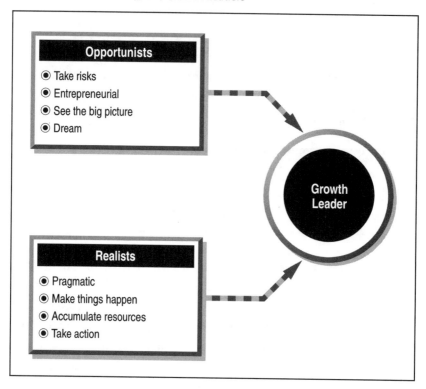

On the other hand, leaders of growth companies must also be realists—they must consider an opportunity for what it *could be* rather than what they *wish it to be*. It's OK to dream—and effective leaders of growth champions have the ability to identify great entrepreneurial growth opportunities. But these same leaders must also see if these opportunities are feasible and have the possibility of increasing profitability and ultimately shareholder value. And if a growth opportunity is not currently feasible but offers huge potential benefits, leaders of growth champions figure out what their company must do to gain the skills necessary for pursuing the opportunity. By playing the realist role, leaders of growth companies manage the risks associated with the opportunities they are willing to pursue—*high* risks become *cal-*

culated risks. Also in this role, leaders take action. It is not good enough to simply anticipate needs before customers know the needs exist. Great leaders also have the courage to take action. As a realist, a growth leader will figure out ways to make things happen.

Learning as a Way of Life

How do managers in growth companies actually wear both hats? How can they be both opportunists and realists? An interesting characteristic of growth-oriented managers is that they are always in a learning mode, and it is the way in which they learn that allows them to play a dual role. They have formalized processes to gather information that allows them to continually identify new opportunities. A key factor that differentiates leaders of growth champions from typical managers is their willingness to adapt their learning mode to discover a necessary piece of information. There are basically three different modes of learning that have been found in the leaders of growth champions:[1]

1. *Big-picture learning.* This holistic approach to learning is used to conceptualize opportunities. It is similar to the way a child would approach a new discovery—eyes wide open, taking in everything with no preconceived biases. Big-picture learning allows leaders to play the opportunist role.

2. *Pragmatic learning.* This type of learning is very action oriented, where leaders try to find ways to ramp up operations to meet new opportunities and manage growth. Pragmatic learning allows leaders to play the realist role.

3. *Continuous improvement learning.* This type of learning provides ongoing management. It ensures that the op-

portunity develops as expected and that growth is positively impacting the organization. Remember that effective leaders not only initiate action—they take the steps necessary to maintain action.

United We Stand: Top Management Teams as a Catalyst for Growth

What makes a good leader? Is it an art or a science? Can it be learned or are great leaders born with the ability to lead? Unfortunately, many of the books on leadership still focus on a single leader, namely the CEO—a very limited view of leadership.

Ironically, leadership in most growth companies results from the collective actions of individuals working as a team that turn strategies into action, that make dreams become realities. Leadership goes far beyond an individual leader. Leadership occurs at every level in an organization. Even at the highest level in a company, it is usually the top management team that makes key decisions, not the individual CEO. So when designing a top management team, who should be involved and to what extent are integral leadership issues for successfully growing a company. Specifically coordinating a group of growth specialists, each with different skills, will create and sustain growth.

There Is No "I" In "Team"

Do top management teams really matter or is it the CEO? Admittedly, the answer is both: It's the CEO who manages the top management team, but the more a company institutes such practices as participate management, empowerment, delegation, and teaming, the more important top management teams become relative to a single leader. I have been fortunate to work with many outstanding leaders, most of whom are up front in admitting that it is not their individual efforts that make things happen but rather a combined effort of their top management team—a set of players that affects the organization's performance. John Chambers, CEO of Cisco Systems, sums it up nicely: "[A] key element of a leader is how good is your team. If you ask 'What's going to get the result?' it is actually the quality of the team that is the key determining factor."[2] Regardless of whether you are the CEO of a large multinational, a manager of a division with that large multinational, or a leader of a start-up dot-com, your team will determine your success.

In a growth study I performed by interviewing thousands of executives from over 200 companies, it was a top-management-team characteristic (functional diversity, discussed later in this chapter) that had more of an impact on top-line growth and bottom-line profit than a company's market characteristics.[3] Moreover, when testing the simultaneous impact of market factors, top-management-team factors, and strategy factors, the combined impact of top management teams had more influence in predicting growth than markets and strategies.[4] This may help explain why growth champions continually figure out ways to grow, even when their markets aren't.

In the Sibson & Company study of growth companies noted in the last chapter, it was also found that growth companies that believed their top management teams had more talent than competitors outperformed average companies by almost 70 percent in terms of shareholder value over a ten-year time frame. As one CEO from the study put it, "The greatest obstacle to our growth is having a sufficient number of outstanding managers to attack the [growth] opportunities before us."[5]

_____

Stacking the Deck: Putting Together a Great Top Management Team

Tom Peters recently stated that in order to put together a winning team, you need to think like the general manager of an NBA team.[6] You have 12 seats you need to fill with the hottest talent you can draft; if a new member of the top management team doesn't significantly improve the team, that person should probably not be added. Remember, when constructing a winning top management team, adequate isn't good enough.

At General Electric, Jack Welch refers to members of his top management team as "A" players. Welch states that there is "a unique brand of 21st-century business leader—the GE A player." To be an A player, according to Welch, a manager must embody the four Es:

1. *Energy.* Effective leaders need a high level of energy to create and manage growth.

2. *Energize.* Not only should effective leaders have a high level of energy themselves, but they should also be able to energize others.

3. *Edge.* Managers of growth companies need the ability to make tough calls.

4. *Execute.* Managers of growth companies must have consistent ability to turn a vision into results.

Welch attributes GE's success to the quality of his top management team. "These A players, driving [GE's] initiatives, have transformed the very nature of GE—what it does and how quickly it does it."

Jeff Bezos, founder and chief executive officer of Amazon.com, also recognizes the extraordinary talent of his top management team. His ability to stack the deck has allowed him to create the world's largest online department store. Initially, he hired Joe Galli from Black & Decker to be his COO, Warren Jenson from Delta Airlines to be his CFO, and the top logistics team from Wal-Mart to set up his leading-edge logistics network to provide customers with a one-stop shop for numerous purchasing needs. It was the combined effort of Amazon's top management team that catapulted it to the front line of one of the hottest growth opportunities in the history of business.

Finding "A" Players

How can a company find the managerial talent it needs to create and sustain growth? McKinsey and Sibson performed a joint research project to answer this question.[7] A company can rely on three fundamental principals to obtain great players for its top management team:

1. *Don't forget you get what you pay for.* Managers provide value to companies; companies provide value to managers. Managers can guide a company to value innovation, growth, and profitability by combining intellectual capital and effort. Similarly, companies provide numerous benefits to managers: a good working environment, an opportunity for creative expression, flexibility, and a means of income. It all comes down to a value exchange between managers and their company. Companies that provide a better value exchange will attract better managers. As Bill Gray, senior VP of human resources at Harley Davidson, states, "We don't own our employees. They lend us their intellectual capital and we must pay a fair return or they will deploy their capital elsewhere." Growth champions know the value of great management and they reward accordingly.

2. *Enforce accountability.* Building a talented management team isn't easy. One of the best ways to create talent is to make the *team* responsible for attracting and nurturing talent. Companies that successfully develop talent create metrics for measuring that talent similarly to the way most companies use traditional measures to assess financial performance. And the winners in the talent game are not shy about raising the bar. If someone doesn't stack up or perform at a high level, he or she is gone. Adequate isn't good enough.

3. *Invest in human capital the same way you'd invest in any other type of capital.* When a company invests in capital, it expects to achieve a certain level of return. Growth companies use this same mentality for investing in human capital. As companies invest in human capital, they expect metrics such as customer satisfaction and the bottom line to improve. Numerous companies have seen improvements in employee satisfaction lead to decreased turnover and decreased absenteeism that in turn lead to an improvement in bottom-line profits.

Managing Egos

One difficulty that seems to challenge leaders of growth companies more than leaders of average companies is controlling the egos of its managers. It is not uncommon for past success to lead to overconfidence and ultimately the pursuit of some unjustifiable risky opportunities. Leaders of growth champions need to be aware that a result of having a team of A players creates the possibility for arrogance, which in turn leads to complacency.

At GE, Jack Welch knows that arrogance has caused other growth champions to stumble. He makes a concerted effort to ensure that managers at GE are confident but not cocky. As a company achieves the type of success that GE has achieved in the last decade, maintaining confidence while managing arrogance is a difficult challenge. As Welch puts it, "History points a warning finger toward arrogance and complacency."

Diversity: The Key to a Winning Top Management Team

What types of A players should you look for? How important are their backgrounds and experience? How should they interact with the rest of the top management team to produce the best results? Studies of top management teams have identified diversity as the single most important top-management-team attribute for achieving organizational growth.[8]

Information centered on the importance of diversity in organizations can be found in abundance. Diversity is a critical attribute in trying to assemble a top management team to lead a growth company: it encourages creativity and offers different opinions; it creates constructive conflict; and it improves the chance of a management team's success by reducing tendencies toward complacency.

Setting the Mood

Growth champions encourage and actively consider a wide range of opinions from top-management-team members. But how can growth champions create an environment for diversity? First, there must be a genuine encouragement of different and divergent viewpoints and perspectives. Although most people don't welcome managers who always seem to take a different spin on a topic or issue, growth companies embrace them. Most people view the manager who always seems to challenge conventional approaches and asks the "what if" questions as a burden. Yet this is precisely the type of diversity that impacts growth positively. Diversity of ideas is the springboard of creativity.

In addition to encouraging diverse opinions, top management teams must actively consider, thoroughly ponder, and equitably weigh diverse ideas. Top management teams of growth champions are consistent in terms of avoiding the temptation to dismiss diverse opinions (a suggestion easier said than done). It falls largely on the entire management team's shoulders to demonstrate a respectful and positive approach toward diversity in order to unleash its creative potential.

One of the best ways for a growth business to affirm that it has sufficient diversity is to ensure that the top management team is comprised of individuals with varied sets of skills. This team may include members with rich management experience, extensive field exposure, or a heavy marketing emphasis. It takes a lot of strength to look in the mirror and critically evaluate your top management team and even more strength to actually take action to fill unmet needs. Consider the creative energies of Yahoo! founders Jerry Yang and David Filo. Yang and Filo recognized early opportunities as Internet use was beginning to grow. Yet they were astute enough to know that they had certain deficiencies in their business skills. Therefore, they actively recruited more seasoned managers who developed many of the strategies that led to the business's phenomenal growth and success. Hiring Timothy Koogle as CEO and Jeffrey Mallett as COO brought new approaches, such as upbeat marketing campaigns and charging fees to advertisers. These newcomers to its top management team helped transform Yahoo! from a basic Internet directory into a pivotal hub of Internet activity.

FIGURE 5.2   Types of Diversity for Top Management Teams

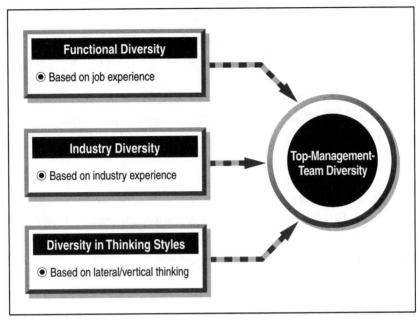

Defining Diversity

By now, I hope you are buying that diversity in the top management team is an important ingredient in a growth champion's success. When working with a client, it's right about now that I hear, "Wait a minute, what do you mean by diversity?" This is a wonderful question because diversity has been defined in many different ways. But how do growth champions define diversity? Many design their top management team around three diversity characteristics as shown in Figure 5.2.

Diversity in functional background. Diversity in functional background refers to different backgrounds of the top-management-team members in their functional areas of expertise. These areas are based on specific aspects of a person's job-related activities. For example, top-management-team members may have expertise in a variety of such functional areas as marketing, operations, accounting and finance, research and development, or human resources management.

In my studies of growth champions, I have found diversity of functional experience to be the single most important type of diversity for growth-oriented top management teams. Functional diversity can produce constructive conflict where team members with different functional backgrounds provide a system of checks and balances in decision making. For example, top-management-team members with heavy R&D experience will not be allowed to allocate an overly large percentage of capital to research if they are competing with marketing for resources. Similarly, a top-management-team member with an extensive accounting background will usually place considerable emphasis on staying within budget.

Diversity in industry experience. Diversity in industry experience results in better decision making because members with many years in a particular industry can offer insights based on their rich experience, whereas newcomers can provide fresh ideas. For example, over the years a top-management-team member with experience may develop a solid understanding of consumer needs. A newcomer can provide an outside perspective that a tenured executive may overlook or may see interrelationships or opportunities that may have never crossed the minds of an old-timer. Each type of perspective is beneficial. Combining the expertise of experienced managers with fresh ideas from relatively new managers provides top management teams the best of both worlds.

Diversity in Thinking Styles: Lateral versus Vertical Thinking. Growth champions intentionally try to find individuals with different thinking styles when constructing a top management team.

Lateral Thinkers	Vertical Thinkers
Big picture–oriented	Detail oriented
Produce divergent possibilities	Proceed logically and carefully
Challenge rules	Follow rules
Catalysts for new ideas	Focus on small improvements
Remove imposed constraints . . .	Work within given constraints

Lateral thinkers are imaginative, coming up with some great, albeit off-the-wall, ideas. They are creative but may not have the ability to get the job done. They may not be able to motivate others to make things happen. Conversely, managers who are great at detail-oriented tasks (vertical thinkers) get things done by taking actions. Unfortunately, many times they don't have the ability to step back and see the big picture. So by having a mix of lateral and vertical thinkers, growth champions are able to achieve balance between these two types of thinkers. The result is a top management team that is good at both dreaming and doing and thus supporting the CEO's dual role of opportunist and realist.

Size of the Top Management Team

Often I'm asked how large should a top management team be. I wish I had a definitive answer. Unfortunately, every situation is so different that providing a magic number would probably do more harm than good. So rather than trying to come up with a specific number, I usually stress the importance of understanding the advantages and disadvantages associated with having a well-balanced top management team versus a top management team that is too small or a top management team that is too large. From this discussion you should get a pretty good idea of an effective range for your own company.

Two conflicting perspectives have worked their way into the management advice pipeline on the impact of top-management-team size on business growth. One perspective contends that larger top management teams enable decision makers to specialize and make faster decisions to positively impact organizational growth. Conversely, others have suggested that larger top management teams create more discussion that slows decision making and results in disharmony.

I have worked with top management teams that had as few as 3 members to some with as many as 18 members. Clearly there are disadvantages associated with both extremes; therefore, most growth champions avoid these extremes. A 3-member team won't generate enough discussion nor have the potential for diversity that is needed for creativity. An extremely large team of 18 members will slow down decision making and therefore hurt responsiveness. Most successful growth companies that I have encountered have top management teams ranging from 6 to 10 members. These teams are large enough to generate creative, diverse ideas but small enough to make decisions quickly.

Pushing Down Leadership: Encouraging Growth Domains

Growth champions are very effective at pushing leadership down to lower levels to create growth domains within their organization by communicating (at all levels of the business) the top management team's commitment to growth.

Emerson Electric's largest division generates annual sales in excess of $1.5 billion. Recently the division spent $300 million to perfect a chip technology known as the "compliant scroll." It looks like a child's spinning wheel, but the device allows compressors to operate more efficiently and much quieter. Sales of the chip are growing more than 40 percent a year. How did this growth domain evolve? Chuck Knight, Emerson's CEO, is excellent at taking his growth vision and pushing it down the organization, creating growth leaders at all levels. Division Vice President Howard Lance admits, "Before, some of these projects would have been taken off the table. People would say 'Oh, Chuck won't want to talk about that.' Now we talk about it, because we all know we're pushing for growth."[9] Knight has been very effective at communicating his growth vision to the rest of the company. Great leaders have the ability to communicate their intentions to everyone in the company. The better they can communicate, the more likely growth opportunities will start popping up.

Pepsi-Cola of North America has focused considerable efforts on ensuring that every employee, at every level, understands why the company is pursuing dramatic expansion into waters, juices, and other beverages. Pepsi's executives make a concerted effort to explain to employees how the cola industry has matured and that the key to future growth for the company is through aggressive product line expansion.

Creating Leaders at All Levels through Effective Communication

A casual observer may think that open communication applies to communication activities among top-management-team members and/or between the top management team and their employees. Many growth champions know that communication doesn't stop there. They must also be willing and able to listen carefully to key customers and employees who are able to spot new growth opportunities. No company is too large or bureaucratic that top management cannot listen to these groups. When a company is market driven, it is always playing catch-up, reacting to customer demands. As noted in previous chapters, growth companies anticipate needs to stay ahead of customers. If a top management team can develop that type of mentality—carefully listening to key stakeholders—the company will be way ahead of its competition.

Growth champions know that communication should be open in two directions; planning requires both top-down and bottom-up communication. To get the most benefit from bottom-up communication, a top management team should understand that different functional areas in the company can each provide unique information. For example, salespeople in the field may provide input that directly feeds back into the top management team's opportunist role by providing it with ideas that may turn into new growth opportunities. These same salespeople can also transmit information that feeds back into the top management team's realist role. If salespeople indicate that orders are behind and customers are becoming upset, the company needs to focus on ramping up to meet demand.

Top management teams of growth champions are particularly good at encouraging an upward flow of ideas from employees. By encouraging these ideas, organizations become more creative and ultimately innovative. In addition, when a top management team provides an environment that encourages the expression of ideas, workers become more involved and satisfied. In the United States, however, companies have not been very successful at encouraging suggestions from employees. The following table illustrates findings from the Japanese Human Relations Association.

Company	Annual Suggestions per Employee
Tohoku Oki	833.2
Mazda	126.5
Fuji Electric	99.6
Matsushita	79.6
Canon	78.1
Hitachi	63.4
JVC	48.6

Toyota	47.6
Nippon Denso	41.6
Nissan	38.5
Leading U.S. companies	2.3

Clearly, Japanese top managers are excellent at encouraging the upward flow of ideas. Idea generation is everybody's business and so, ultimately, is growth. This is the principle growth champions use to push leadership down to lower levels.

Where average U.S. companies are not very effective in encouraging feedback from employees, growth champions excel at assuring that an upward flow of information is utilized. Hewlett-Packard is an example of a growth champion that successfully encourages an upward flow of ideas. The top management team accomplishes upward feedback in three different ways: (1) management by objectives; (2) an open-door policy; and (3) encouraging open communication.

1. *Management by objectives.* Even though management by objectives (MBO) has fallen out of favor with most companies, H-P uses it so that individuals at each level contribute to company goals by developing objectives that are integrated with their manager's. H-P believes that MBO contributes to flexibility and innovation by recognizing alternative approaches to meeting objectives. Ultimately, the company credits MBO with providing an effective means of meeting customer needs. MBO is documented in written plans that guide and create accountability throughout the organization. H-P also uses MBO as a tool for coordination of cross-organizational integration.

2. *Open-door policy.* To encourage upward communication at H-P, an open-door policy is strongly enforced. This policy provides assurance that no adverse conse-

quences will result when employees responsibly raise issues with management or personnel. H-P's open-door policy is effective because it is built on trust and integrity between employees and management. It provides an environment for workers to share feelings and frustrations in a constructive manner. And in addition, H-P's open-door policy is useful for clearing up communication breakdowns.

3. *Open communication.* At the core of H-P's practice of open communication is the belief that when given the right tools, training, and information to do a good job, people will contribute their best. H-P credits its open communication environment to strong teamwork between H-P people and customers, resulting in customer relationships built on trust and respect.

Maintaining the Momentum: Issues of Growth in Human Resource Management

I have often heard successful managers say that the best way to achieve success is to surround yourself with talented employees. However, actually pulling this off may not be as easy as it sounds. According to a recent survey of growth companies performed by PricewaterhouseCoopers, 65 percent of all CEOs of growth companies say that the lack of skilled workers available is the number one barrier to growth.

Employee education and development can help to overcome this problem. Several studies have shown that a 10 percent increase in education of existing employees is much more significant in improving bottom-line performance than increasing work hours by 10 percent. In addition, employee education and development increase employees' organizational commitment and reduce turnover. A recent study by the National Center of

Educational Quality found that workers who received as few as six days of annual training a year were significantly more satisfied than those who received fewer or none.

In fast-growth companies, people don't always grow as fast as the company. As a company grows, long-term managers who have been with the company for years may find themselves in over their heads, trying to manage businesses for which they don't have the skills. Although you hope they will be able to grow into the job, the reality is they are already overworked and probably don't have the time, energy, and possibly skills to learn their new role. They often excelled at achieving past goals (e.g., cost cutting), but they don't know how to grow a business. One of two things usually results. Ideally, the company will train its employees and bring them up to speed in their new role, but often the employees become so frustrated with a new job that they end up quitting.

Finding Talent

Successfully attracting top-management-team talent also applies to talented employees at lower levels. However, many companies think of hiring talent as the ability to hire individuals with cutting-edge expertise. Growth companies realize that talent comes in many forms. Even in a high-tech company like Netscape, hiring talent focuses more on management than on technical expertise. Jim Clark and Marc Andreessen made a conscious effort to attract talent in the form of managerial experience to complement the company's technically talented individuals.

Developing Talent

The continual shortage of talent, previously noted, constrains many companies in their efforts to achieve growth.

Growth champions, in contrast, excel at developing talent. They provide the resources and support necessary for growing talent within their own company and remove roadblocks that may impede the nurturing of talent.

Because these companies are moving at such a fast pace, they typically have fewer formal processes in place. Many growth champions hold their teams accountable for developing talent. The teams develop metrics for talent just as they would develop measures for financial performance. GE has a noteworthy model for developing talented employees. It is especially effective in pruning managers at top levels by moving out average managers to make room for outstanding managers, which allows GE to continually raise the bar for talented managers.

Under the Gun: Finding Experience versus Gaining Experience

When a company experiences fast growth, it's often difficult to groom and develop green employees into effective leaders because it just doesn't have the time. Given Netscape's incredible pace of growth, its strategy is to hire people who can hit the ground running and it doesn't hire many new graduates. Netscape uses this strategy for all levels of management. It looks for people who have already proven themselves, who have already done the job that Netscape is hiring them for. Many companies take the position that they don't want to hire employees who are set in their ways, but Netscape puts priority on experience. It feels that by hiring people who already have solid work experience, it actually saves money that would otherwise be invested in training and development.

Netscape's strategy does have its drawbacks. The biggest downside to hiring people with considerable experience rather than a new college graduate is "sticker price." Put bluntly, you get what you pay for. The more experience someone has, the higher the compensation package to attract that person to your company. Netscape had to be one of the compensation leaders in Silicon Valley to attract its managers.

Big Brothers, Big Sisters: Baptism by Fire through Mentoring

As new employees come into a fast-growth organization, not only does management have to be concerned with maintaining culture (discussed in Chapter 4), it should be concerned with maintaining day-to-day operational activities. If a company experiences hypergrowth, it is difficult to have new employees understand how to get things done.

At Tactics, an Atlanta-based technology firm specializing in Oracle applications, seasoned employees (some of the "seasoned" employees have been there less than a year) spend considerable time mentoring new employees. Mentoring is a very effective way to indoctrinate new employees into a fast-growth company. Tactics' mentoring is not simply a one-on-one program; rather, it's a many-on-many program. New employees have the flexibility to ask any coworker to oversee their work. Similarly, senior managers often bring new employees to customers' facilities where they can learn by doing. The company stresses this approach because it encourages skill sharing, the ability of new employees to learn from seasoned veterans. Unfortunately, at many consulting firms mentoring is not very effective. As a consultant learns a new skill, he or she is hesitant to share this new found knowledge with other employees because it increases others' marketability as high-profile jobs open up. To overcome this problem, some companies are now creating reward systems to encourage employees to share knowledge and skills with peers.

Endnotes

1. Peter Lorange, "Strategy Implementation: The New Realities, *Long Range Planning* 31, no. 1 (1998): 18–29.

2. Scott Thurm, "How to Drive an Express Train: At Fast-Moving Cisco, CEO Says Put Customers First, View Rivals as 'Good Guys'," *Wall Street Journal*, (June 1, 2000): B1.

3. Laurence G. Weinzimmer, "A Replication and Extension of Organizational Growth Determinants," *Journal of Business Research* 48, no. 1 (2000): 33–42.

4. Laurence G. Weinzimmer, Paul C. Nystrom, and Sarah J. Freeman, "Methods for Measuring Organizational Growth: Issues, Consequences, and Contingencies," *Journal of Management* 24, no. 2 (1998): 235–62.

5. Jude T. Rich, "The Growth Imperative," *Journal of Business Strategy* (March/April 1999): 27–31.

6. Tom Peters, "The Wow Project," *Fast Company* 24 (1999): 116–27.

7. Rich, "The Growth Imperative."

8. Laurence G. Weinzimmer, "Top Management Team Determinants of Organizational Growth in a Small Business Context: A Comparative Study," *Journal of Small Business Management* 35, no. 3 (1997): 1–10.

9. Ronald Henkoff, "Growing Your Company: Five Ways to Do It Right!" *Fortune* (November 25, 1996): 78–85.

THREE

Strategy Catalysts
The Marriage of Markets and Capabilities

*M*any great opportunities are lost because no one is willing to make the first move, to take the risk, to actually do something instead of just talking about doing it. Creating effective growth strategies initiates action; it allows a company to use its capabilities to exploit growth opportunities.

Unfortunately, too many companies continually focus on getting a bigger piece of the pie (conventional competitive strategy). Sooner or later the pie will run out and so will future growth opportunities. Although most average companies limit themselves by their self-imposed definition of a competitive market—by the size of their pie—growth champions don't assume that it must be the right way just because everyone else does it that way. Instead, they create strategies that innovate value by offering total solutions to customer needs.

I'll discuss how successful companies are able to generate numerous growth opportunities regardless of their markets. And I'll explain how growth champions create strategies to avoid becoming one-hit wonders.

In this section, I'll also explore the three different types of relationship strategies. Each has distinct advantages and disadvantages. An effective manager has to become familiar with all three choices as well as with the factors that determine which relationship strategy is most appropriate in a given situation.

6

Growing at E-Speed

Strategies for Creating instead of Competing

After you've spent countless hours creating and identifying fast-growth opportunities and agonizing over assessments of how your business stacks up to these opportunities, it's time for a payoff. *Strategy development* is the means to that end. It determines how you will exploit growth opportunities and provides the critical link between fast-growth opportunities and organizational capabilities.

The numerous books that have been written about strategy development have suggested several strategic choices: (1) competitive-level strategies (how to compete within a defined industry); (2) diversification strategies (deciding what industries to compete in); (3) entry-level strategies (how to enter a given industry); and (4) competitive-level tactics (gaining and protecting market share in a given industry). What all of these strategy definitions have in common is their focus on *competition* by relying on artificial boundaries used to define competitive industries. Growth champions don't pay attention to artificial boundaries; they create value for customers.

Rather than trying to figure out what each of these strategy permutations can contribute to growing your business and then coming up with some grand strategic design, let's simplify things. Recall from Chapter 2 that there are two basic types of growth opportunities:

1. *Incremental-growth opportunities* are based on conventional strategic thinking and often result from minor improvements to something a company already does.

2. *Leap-growth opportunities* are often radical, challenging conventional strategic thought.

Consequently, growth companies pursue two basic types of strategies. Incremental-growth strategies are designed to pursue growth opportunities by doing what you are currently doing, only a little better. They are designed to try to get a bigger piece of the pie, focusing on increasing market share in some finite industry. In contrast, leap-growth strategies center on value innovation. Rather than focusing on competition to get a bigger piece of the pie, leap-growth strategies focus on ways to make the pie bigger, allowing for significant long-term growth opportunities. Growth champions manage to achieve an extraordinary balance between these two types of strategies. Incremental-growth strategies provide them stability and the capital to fuel the fire, whereas leap-growth strategies provide sufficient future growth. Pursuing one type of strategy without the other simply won't cut it. You need to simultaneously pursue both types of strategies to achieve sustainable growth.

Focusing exclusively on incremental-growth strategies is common in most average companies. Rather than looking beyond their competition, they are overburdened with the thought of trying to keep up with the Joneses. They rarely achieve significant growth, and, if they do, it is usually only short-lived. Trying to achieve sustainable growth without incorporating leap-growth strategies is like trying to fly a kite without any wind. You keep running and running, tugging the kite behind you, only to have it continually crash to the ground. If you only had a gust of wind to get the kite above the tree line, but that gust of wind never comes, and you keep running and running, but never succeed. Similarly, pursuing incremental-growth strategies without leap-growth strategies never gets you above the tree line—it may lead to long-term survival, but it won't lead to long-term growth.

At the other end of the spectrum are companies that focus only on leap-growth strategies. These companies are always looking for the big hit, a get-rich-quick opportunity. If one of these companies hits it big, it usually ends up being a one-hit wonder, going to the top of the charts for a short period of time and then mysteriously vanishing.

Incremental-growth strategies keep a company plodding along at a steady pace while leap-growth strategies create huge opportunities to realize significant benefits. Growth champions benefit from the stability of incremental-growth strategies to cover the risks associated with pursuing leap-growth strategies. To win the race, you need the consistency of the tortoise and the speed of the hare.

Incremental-Growth Strategies: Playing Follow-the-Leader for a Bigger Piece of Pie

Why do we hear so much in the strategy literature about competition? We are bombarded with notions of competitive strategies, competitive advantage, competitive intelligence, and competitive pressures. We are told time and again that to be successful, a company must focus on competition and do whatever is necessary to squeeze a few tenths of a percentage point of market share away from competitors. This only leads to a downward spiral because we get caught up in a zero-sum game (in order for us to win, they have to lose). We tend to imitate, to become in-grained with a me-too attitude. We end up striving for mediocrity, thinking average is good enough, reacting to competitive circumstances as they come. For growth champions, average is never good enough.

Remember the game follow-the-leader? Well, odds are, you continue to play this child's game with your business. Or even worse, you may find yourself in a game of follow-the-follower, never asking yourself if the companies you compete with are successful enough to use as role models. It's a very subtle trap, often evolving over years and years of continual focus on competition. But here we find ourselves drifting aimlessly along in a great sea of competition—ships without rudders, dependent on the tides, hoping that somehow we will end up a winner.

I'm not suggesting you should forget about competition—that would be foolish. But limiting your future to being part of the crowd doesn't hold a lot of promise. Moreover, given the myriad of rapid changes emanating from improved business models and the new economy, you may find yourself expending considerable effort trying to understand and react to your competition, only to be blindsided by an aspiring dot-com. Even assuming competition is moving forward, it is virtually impossible to make sufficient gains by playing follow-the-leader with competitors. Instead, growth champions move beyond a competitive mind-set.

The point here is simple: think beyond what you hear in traditional strategy literature to achieve leap growth. While you need to develop some advantages over your competitors to be successful in your marketplace, there's much more than incrementally crawling along playing the me-too game. Growth champions know that successfully innovating value is not the result of focusing on competition.

Value innovation comes from *creating* rather than *competing*.

Conventional Competitive Strategy: The Basis of Incremental Growth

Is there any value to conventional competitive strategy? If so, what can we take from current strategic thought? Are there any benefits to focusing on our competitive environment?

The answer to all of these questions is a resounding yes. A very important ingredient in putting together a balanced plan for long-term success comes from competitive strategy: incremental growth. Incremental-growth strategies, as noted previously, fall in the category of what I call traditional strategic thinking. Companies focus on competitors' products and strategies and many times battle for small gains in market share. Incremental-growth strategies are very effective in linking a business to its competitive environment. These strategies are predictable, expose a company to minimal risk, and can keep a business above water for an indefinite period of time. While these strategies are important, they are only a small part of the big picture.

Incremental-growth strategies rarely yield significant growth for a business. The source of incremental growth comes in one of two forms:

1. *Low-cost strategies*—competing on price, based on advantageous cost position relative to competition

2. *Differentiation strategies*—competing on uniqueness, based on some platform that makes a company's products/services different relative to competitors

Each competitive-level strategy has different requirements, as seen in Figure 6.1.

Low Cost. From traditional strategy literature, the first competitive choice a firm can pursue is based on low-cost advantages. In this instance, a company tries to minimize its cost base

---

FIGURE 6.1   Requirements for Effective Competitive-Level Strategies

	Low Cost	Differentiation
Markets	Broad based	Segmented
Products	Simple/Commodity	Complex
Capabilities	Operations expertise Process R&D	Marketing Product R&D

as much as possible to compete on price. Companies that compete based on cost often serve very broad-based undifferentiated markets, attempting to sell the same product/service to everyone, regardless of the customer's background. The ability to offer a similar product to every customer creates significant economies of scale, consequently lowering the companies' cost base. Products are usually very simple. The simpler the product, the lower the cost base. Finally, companies that compete on cost have considerable expertise in process technology, operations and/or supply-chain management. Note in Figure 6.2 that initially a company can significantly reduce costs as it acquires operations expertise (e.g., improved production flows, cell manufacturing, etc.).

At a certain point, however, it becomes difficult to reduce costs any further—they can only be reduced so much. As the cost curve begins to flatten out, competitors have a chance to catch up.

Is a low-cost strategy effective for maintaining sustainable growth? While managing cost is important for any business, low-cost strategies usually won't lead to long-term growth.

FIGURE 6.2   Relationship between Operations Expertise and Cost

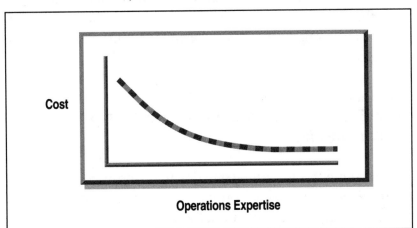

Differentiation. Rather than competing on cost, firms that choose differentiation as a competitive-level strategy compete on uniqueness. They usually serve segmented markets (the more unusual the product or service, the less appealing it is to a broad-based market). Products are usually more complex because the more complex the product, the easier it is to differentiate. Firms can differentiate by creating new and unique products or by convincing consumers via effective marketing that the product is truly unique. The best differentiators capitalize on both product R&D and marketing.

The Realities of Incremental Growth

Incremental growth is based on continuity and therefore provides consistency. Companies that pursue fast growth need an element of consistency. That's the good news. Unfortunately, low-cost and differentiation strategies rarely lead to significant growth. Companies that use these strategies are market driven, reacting to changes in the marketplace. In contrast to most companies, growth champions generate growth a different way.

Rather than being market driven, they are market drivers. Rather than settling for incremental growth, they pursue leap growth. Although incremental-growth strategies have been around for a long time, there is surprisingly little discussion of leap-growth strategies . . . anywhere.

Leap-Growth Strategies: Driving Markets to Expand the Pie

Incremental-growth strategies focus on winning market share away from competition, getting a bigger piece of the pie. If a management team continually focuses on getting a bigger piece of the pie, sooner or later the pie will run out and their company will hit a wall. Many average companies limit themselves by their self-imposed definition of a competitive market, by the size of their pie. In contrast, growth champions don't limit themselves to artificial, predetermined constraints we know as market boundaries. Growth companies know that the only way to grow over the long term is to expand their pie. Rather than spending all of their energy trying to outmaneuver competitors, fast-growth companies figure out ways to make the pie bigger. The larger the pie becomes, the greater the growth opportunities.

How do they do it? How do growth champions expand their boundaries to pursue new (and appropriate) growth opportunities? Rather than focusing on competition, they focus on value creation. Rather than focusing exclusively on incremental-growth strategies, they also focus on leap-growth strategies.

Leap-growth strategies are radical. They are aggressive strategies that focus on value innovation rather than traditional competition. Here's a key attribute that separates growth champions from ordinary companies:

> *A*verage companies race to beat competition. Fast-growth companies make competition less important by providing customers with innovations in value.

This doesn't mean that you need to contact a psychic or brilliant futurist to help your business grow. What it does mean is that you have a solid understanding of your markets and customers' needs and then will figure out ways to fulfill those needs.

Consider Xpedior Inc., one of the premier e-business consulting firms in the world. Xpedior's CEO, David Campbell, isn't content to simply keep pace with competitors in the Internet consulting market. He maintains, "Our intent would be to grow faster than our market," a market that is growing at 60 percent per year. Can Xpedior accomplish this goal by focusing on competitors? Clearly the answer is no. That does not mean that Xpedior ignores competition. Xpedior Vice President Jackie Lefton notes, "One has simply to open an Internet publication to know we have several strong competitors." However, Xpedior doesn't follow in the footsteps of its competitors; its primary focus is on value innovation. The company realizes that technology must be complemented by creativity to provide leading-edge strategic solutions for clients, and competitors realize this too.

To move ahead of competition rather than just keeping pace with it, Xpedior provides total solutions to clients by understanding their needs better than anyone else. Most companies in the end-to-end e-business consulting market focus exclusively on trying to develop new technologies. Xpedior has taken e-business consulting much further. Even though the company does have leading-edge technical solutions, given the uncertainties associated with rapid changes in the e-business consulting market, customers need much more than leading-edge technology. Based on customer responses, Lefton credits much of Xpedior's success to the company's ability to satisfy four additional value drivers:

1. *Integrity*—based on experience and the ability to understand its customers' businesses

2. *Commitment*—to do whatever it takes to ensure that clients' businesses are successful

3. *Relationships*—to ensure long-term success

4. *Risk sharing*—having the willingness to share and even assume clients' risks

Has an unparalleled focus on value innovation rather than on competition created leap growth for Xpedior? In 1999, the company grew 85.3 percent and in the second quarter of 2000, revenue growth exceeded 100 percent. Campbell has realized his intent of growing faster than the market.

The Nature of Leap-Growth strategies

Leap-growth strategies are more difficult to develop compared with incremental-growth strategies. Because they are radical, leap-growth opportunities are often somewhat elusive to most businesspeople. Consequently, there is more risk associated with leap-growth strategies.

To achieve leap growth, growth champions break away from the crowd. While they recognize competition, that is not their main focus. In contrast with most companies, growth champions focus on creating value for their customers rather than outperforming competition. They are proactive market drivers, creating value before customers know there's a need rather than reacting (often too late) to changes in the tide. This new school of thought is a natural extension of having an external frame for understanding markets—combining market knowledge with leading-edge internal expertise to identify new growth opportunities. Xpedior has shown us this can be the ability to see new solutions for customers that others don't see and many times requiring the involvement of customers themselves.

It is not surprising that most companies remain competitively based, even though common sense would dictate that successful companies focus on customer value. In a recent study of new venture launches at INSEAD, a leading European university, it was found that 86 percent of new business ventures were competition based and only 14 percent were customer based. However, customer-based business ventures accounted for 38 percent of total revenue and 61 percent of total profit.[1] In other words, value-based, customer-oriented ventures far outperform competitive-based, me-too ventures.

Pierre Teilhard de Chardin states: "It is our duty as men and women to proceed though the limits to our abilities do not exist. We are collaborators in creation." This is the basic difference between those companies that grow and those that retain their status quo. Growth companies push the limits. They are willing to chart out new territories.

Designing Leap-Growth Strategies through Value Innovation

Value innovation is the essence of being a true market driver—it leads to leap growth. Growth champions drive markets proactively as opposed to being market driven. Although a lot of companies talk about value creation, only a select few talk about *value innovation*. Recall from Chapter 2 that value creation and value innovation are not the same. Value creation is usually an incremental improvement over existing products or services and many times is a metric to convince customers that they should pay more. In contrast, value innovatuon is a means of providing total solutions for customers' needs. Many times, value innovators provide solutions for customers before the customers even realize there is a deficient need. I have recently heard a new phrase that relates to value innovation—*new market space*. Advocates of new market space argue that companies need to break away from conventional thinking about competitive strategy (haven't we heard this once or twice already?) and seek out customer value gaps that others seem to ignore or overlook. Companies that win this unoccupied space help to ensure sustainable growth over a long period of time.

In their five-year study of growth companies, Professors W. Chan Kim and Renee Mauborgne define value innovation as (1) offering a new product or service that radically improves value and (2) offering value innovation at an affordable price.[2] They state that offering radically superior value at an extremely high price is like "laying an egg that other companies will hatch." Nicholas Hayel, chairman of SMH Corporation, understood this concept very well and initiated a value innovation for the wristwatch industry. He led the development of a highly functional low-cost quartz watch that also made a fashion statement and gave birth to Swatches. At the time, the Japanese were manufacturing high-precision quartz watches starting at $75. To lure customers away from the Japanese, SMH offered the Swatch at a price of $40 so that customers could buy several as fashion accessories. SMH was the first company to target the youth market by manufacturing watches with vibrant colors and creative artwork. Although accuracy was still an important attribute to this customer segment, style was even more important. Swatches were positioned as watches that make a statement rather than watches that are high-precision timekeepers. Rather than trying to beat competitors by improving accuracy down to nanoseconds, SMH took an external view of the market. The company was able to identify an important need for customers: fashion. In addition, SMH developed an unbeatable cost structure to sell its products at a sufficiently lower price. It celebrated the production of its millionth watch in 1992. Now the Swatch brand has been extended into other style-related accessories, such as sunglasses and pagers.

As we have seen, value innovation does not necessarily translate to high technology. Consider news broadcasting. For many years, the three big television networks—ABC, CBS, and NBC—were so concerned with competition that they had identical formats; all three aired the same types of shows at the same times. Then along came CNN with the goal of creating a radical improvement in value. CNN didn't follow in the footsteps of its predecessors; rather, it provided 24-hour news broadcasts from around the world every day of the year. Quickly, CNN emerged as the world leader in global news broadcasting. Moreover, CNN was able to provide 24 hours of news coverage for about one-fifth the cost of a single hour of network news.

Components of Value Innovation

To benefit from value innovation, it is important to understand the three value considerations that a company can pursue:

1. New products

2. Superior service

3. New distribution channels

Many times, businesses try to define value innovation as one-dimensional. Remember that value innovation hinges on providing total solutions to customer needs at an affordable price.

New products. You can develop a value innovation for products even if you're in a service business. In 1988, Bert Claeys set out to create a new experience for movie goers that resulted in Kinepolis. Kinepolis is the world's first movie megaplex (not a multiplex). Claeys built a facility with 25 screens and 7,600 seats, offering patrons in Brussels a radically superior movie experience. Many of the theaters at the megaplex have more than 7,000 seats, each with so much legroom that you don't have to move when someone passes by. Seats are oversized and theaters have steep slopes so no one has an obstructed view; screens are nearly 100 feet by 30 feet. Most of the theaters have state-of-the-art sound systems, and the screens rest on their own foundations so sound vibrations are not transmitted to the picture. In its first year of operations, Kinepolis won a big piece of the pie with 50 percent of the Belgium movie theater market. It also expanded the pie, growing the entire market by 40 percent. Belgians now refer to a night out at the movies as an evening at the Kinepolis. To top it off, the cost base for operations is below industry averages, as the result of high volume and location outside city limits. Kinepolis is a perfect example of how to create a high-growth opportunity in a market that most people would define as stagnant. Many even argue that the movie industry is declining given the boom in video rentals and cable/satellite television. Claeys has shown that value innovation in a stagnant industry can still create significant growth opportunities.

Superior service. Have you ever stopped to think that it costs more to sell a product or service to a new customer than to an existing one? Studies have shown that it costs around 20 percent less to retain an existing customer as opposed to finding a new customer. Because existing customers already know who you are, you don't have to expend resources to increase brand-name recognition, and you're concerned with maintaining rather than winning brand loyalty.

Innovating value through better service is a key way to increase customer satisfaction that leads to significant growth. Moreover, providing excellent service is a very effective way to retain customers. If growth through better service has so much potential, why don't most companies offer it?

To create value innovation via service, you first have to stop assuming that because everyone does it a certain way, then that must be the right way. We can define service in terms of three critical attributes: quality, simplicity, and comprehensiveness. Growth champions excel at all three types of service attributes. Quality gets most of the attention, but don't forget about the value of simplicity and comprehensiveness. The easier (or simpler) you make it for a customer to purchase your product or service (e.g., less hassle, fewer problems and complexities), the easier it is to win over customers. The more comprehensive, or turnkey, your service, the less likely customers will go somewhere else to satisfy their needs.

Joe Kaplan, president and CEO of Innovative Merchant Solutions, has mastered all three attributes of service, providing top-quality products combined with simplicity and turnkey solutions. Innovative Merchant Solutions has become one of the fastest-growing full-service bankcard processing organizations in the United States by offering outstanding products for its customers. In terms of simplicity, the company is a leader in the development of the Internet/bank interface for bankcard processing. For example, merchants are just a click away from receiving online assistance for their accounts. In 2000, the company created its own bank to provide personalized Internet services. In addition, the company provides comprehensive turnkey solutions for its customers, ranging from processing debit cards to establishing ATM locations. Innovative Merchant Solutions will even provide customers with leading-edge Internet solutions. It has successfully become a one-stop shop for its merchants' bankcard needs.

In terms of creating value via service, Kaplan understands that an integral component of sustainable growth is customer retention through outstanding service. While competitors are busy trying to churn new accounts and then move on to the next new account, Innovate Merchant Solutions focuses on developing long-term relationships with clients. According to Kaplan,

"We achieve success by providing the best customer service in the industry." The company has shown that *partnering with* customers rather than *selling to* customers is what separates growth champions from average companies in this industry.

Kaplan has received the Arthur Andersen Award for "Best Business Practices in Customer Satisfaction" for his innovations in customer service. He has also won the Ernst and Young "Entrepreneur of the Year Award," the U.S. Department of Commerce "Blue Chip Enterprise Award," and the U.S. Association for Small Business and Entrepreneurship's "Corporate Entrepreneur of the Year Award."

The ability to provide value via excellent service has translated directly to the company's performance. During the past several years, Innovative Merchant Solutions (and its predecessor Superior) has doubled in size every year and is projected to be one of the top five players in the bankcard processing industry within the next couple of years.

Bottom line: growth champions serve the customer better than anyone else.

New distribution channels. It seems as though most executives focus on developing new products to innovate value. Then there are insightful companies such as Innovative Merchant Solutions that have innovated value by providing a new twist to the concept of service. And there's still one more (albeit often overlooked) avenue to innovate value: distribution. By reconfiguring distribution channels, businesses that are in mature and stagnant industries can achieve phenomenal growth. Starbucks has done it in the mature coffee industry; Home Depot did it in the hardware industry; and Charles Schwab did it in the securities industry. Identifying a new channel can be an outstanding source for significant growth. As Robert Atkins, director of Mercer Management Consulting, says, "Think about Kraft, P&G, and Nestlé watching Starbucks for so many years stealing market share in coffee but not responding with a retail channel of their own." But Starbucks didn't stop its leap growth via distribution channels with its retail stores. New distribution channels have created additional growth opportunities; for example, United Airlines serves Starbucks coffee as does Barnes and Noble bookstores.

And then there is the mother of value innovation via distribution channels—the Internet—that lowers costs and increases response time. Sitting in my office, I can purchase virtually anything from a rare collectible at eBay.com to an automobile on Autoweb.com 24/7 and often at a lower price than my local retailer's price. Companies like Amazon.com have realized tremendous growth by exploiting the Internet as a distribution channel.

Avoiding the One-Hit Wonder: Filling the Leap-Growth Pipeline

As discussed in earlier chapters, any company has numerous opportunities to grow regardless of its present circumstances. By now you know that one of the keys to sustainable growth is balance. Unfortunately, the downside for many value innovators is that they come up with one great idea and stop. Rather than thinking ahead and trying to develop new ideas to put into the pipeline, they rest on their laurels, enjoying the short-term benefits of having a winner. Rather than becoming growth champions, they become one-hit wonders. They quickly rise to the top of the charts and then disappear as fast as they appeared.

In 1997, bike enthusiasts Stephen W. Simons and Paul Turner were on top of the world. They had founded RockShox Inc., a manufacturer of shock absorbers for bicycles; they loved what they were doing and their company was growing at a tremendous rate. The company was 17 on *Business Week*'s list of hot growth companies. After racing to the top, the company shifted into low gear, coasted for a while, and eventually derailed because management didn't look ahead. Although the company had a great product that provided significant revenues, it stopped innovating after one hit. Unfortunately for RockShox, consumer tastes eventually changed and the mountain bike fad quickly diminished. CEO George Napier admitted, "The company just didn't foresee that mountain bikes would stop growing."

An important characteristic of most growth champions is an understanding of their markets. The better you understand your market, the better the chance that you will see opportunities that others don't even know are there.

> Growth champions are good at understanding markets but are even better at developing an ongoing stream of opportunities.

Growth champions put considerable effort into filling their leap-growth pipelines with new opportunities to innovate value for customers. It is as simple as balance. Use incremental growth to provide stability, go to market with your current leap-growth opportunities (destined to become some of tomorrow's incremental-growth opportunities), and then invest resources to identify and act on future possibilities. And possibilities are endless. For an opportunity to be a viable entry into your leap-growth pipeline, it has to meet three criteria:

1. The market should be able to support significant growth.

2. Your company should have sufficient capabilities to exploit the opportunity either internally or by partnering with another firm.

3. The opportunity is something that makes sense—it fits within your mission.

FIGURE 6.3   Types of Leap-Growth Strategies

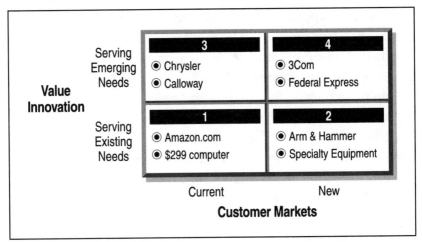

When I was working recently with a group at Caterpillar to develop an aggressive growth plan, we spent considerable time talking about the risks associated with being aggressive. During the discussion, Dan Driscoll, director of marketing communications at Caterpillar, coined the term *rational proactiveness*. A rationally proactive company is a company that can be aggressive as long as managers understand the risks associated with growth and the opportunity seems to be a logical extension of the company's current capabilities. This means that you shouldn't pursue any opportunity just to make money. Trying to be all things to all people is a surefire strategy for disaster.

Types of Leap-Growth Strategies

To fill your pipeline with opportunities, it is important to understand the different types of leap-growth strategies that others have pursued, as seen in Figure 6.3.

Quadrant 1—Creating value for current customers' existing needs. Numerous companies have realized significant leap growth by creating new value for the existing needs of current customers. For example, Amazon.com was already a major player in e-tailing books on the Internet. Customers on Amazon.com are looking for books, and now they have the opportunity to buy other products. The company initiated a way to create additional value for its current customers. Convenience and price were important purchasing drivers for selling books—not the ability to pick up the product and physically touch it. Like its success selling books, Amazon.com has been effective at finding additional products (e.g., CDs, DVDs, software, and video games) that customers don't need to touch before purchasing. Clearly, this is not a new need—Amazon.com just figured out a new way to meet its customers' needs. Similarly, Compaq has created a value innovation for its customers' existing needs. In the summer of 2000, Compaq introduced a $299 computer that customers can use for e-mail and the Internet. Customers already had this need, and Compaq figured out a way for customers to fulfill it more cheaply than by conventional methods.

Quadrant 2—Creating value for new customers' existing needs. Some companies have realized significant growth by figuring out better ways to fulfill customers' needs by moving into new markets. When Arm & Hammer realized that baking soda was useful for absorbing odors, it quickly expanded into several new markets where odor absorption was an issue (e.g., underarm deodorant, toothpaste, carpet cleaners, and laundry detergent). Odor absorption was not a new need for customers; nevertheless, Arm & Hammer just realized how to extend its product into new customer markets.

A high-powered type of leap-growth strategy is extending value innovations via geographical expansion. Serving existing needs in new markets by expanding overseas can lead to significant and sustainable growth. Jeff Rhodenbaugh, president and CEO of Specialty Equipment Company (number 17 in *Business Week*'s 1999 list of hot growth companies) found the U.S. market saturated. The only avenue to growth was through international expansion.

Quadrant 3—Creating a new need for existing customers. Some companies can create a new need for customers. Stated a little differently, some companies have the foresight to fulfill customers' needs before customers realize the need exists. Chrysler did this with the introduction of the minivan, a product that didn't exist until Chrysler introduced it. Minivans filled a gap that no other company had served. Families with children needed the utility of a truck and the comfort of a car. Similarly, Calloway Golf Company introduced titanium drivers to its customers in 1992. Titanium allowed Calloway to increase the size of the head of its golf clubs without increasing the weight. Golfers didn't know they had a need for clubs with bigger heads—Calloway successfully created that need for its current customers.

Quadrant 4—Creating a new need in a new market. A final alternative to achieving leap growth is to create a new need for customers in a totally new market. 3Com was well known for manufacturing computer peripherals such as modems and network peripherals. Then the company created a product to fill a need that customers didn't know existed. With the introduction of the Palm Pilot, 3Com successfully moved into a brand-new market by creating a new need for customers. Fred Smith Jr., founder of Federal Express, also successfully created a new need. Until the mid-1970s, businesses perceived overnight shipping as a luxury service (with the exception of the medical equipment industry). However, by 1980, overnight shipping became a necessity for most companies. And by the mid-1980s, overnight shipping had become the standard for shipping consumer goods as well. Smith literally created a new need.

So leap growth comes in many forms. For a company to maintain significant growth over a long period, it must consider all forms of leap growth as potential areas of expansion. In sum then, growth champions can exploit these different leap-growth opportunities through product creation, superior service, and distribution channels.

Why Growth Companies Are Aggressive

There continues to be an ongoing debate over whether it's better to be aggressive or passive. Clearly, there are benefits with both and risks with both, but it is rare for a passive company to pursue leap growth. If a company decides to aggressively pursue new growth opportunities, it exposes itself to numerous risks. Many business experts contend that companies on the leading edge are also on the "bleeding" edge. They expose themselves to so much risk and invest so much money in leading-edge R&D that someone else may come along and reap the benefits of their hard work. Many times this is exactly what happens; the majority of the time, however, companies taking the leading-edge position reap the rewards.

The benefits and costs associated with being aggressive are illustrated in Figure 6.4. Recognizing that there are both upside and downside risks is an important consideration.

Benefits of Being Aggressive

Success stories of businesses that have taken an aggressive position in pursuing a new growth opportunity are abundant. Three major benefits are possible by being aggressive: brand loyalty; switching costs; and controlling scarce resources.

Brand loyalty. If a company can be aggressive in introducing a new quality product or service, the company can achieve significant brand loyalty. When a company achieves brand loy-

FIGURE 6.4   Benefits and Risks Associated with Being Aggressive

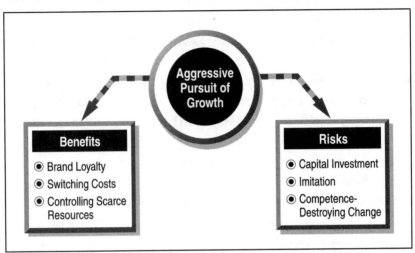

alty, it may deter potential competitors from entering the market. Norwegian-based Nokia has been very aggressive in introducing its digital cell phones; its aggressive market entry has paid off well for Nokia. Recently, Nokia overtook Motorola as the top company in the cell phone industry, owning 27 percent of the U.S. market in 1999; and Nokia is estimated to have the 11th most valuable brand in the world. The company has achieved consistent growth over the last several years, increasing revenues last year by 48 percent, profits by 56 percent, and earnings per share by 51 percent.

Switching costs. If a company aggressively commercializes a new product or service, customers may become a captive audience to that producer. As new versions of a product are introduced, customers have no choice but to buy from the same company they had bought from in the past.

An example of this phenomenon is DOS-based software manufacturing. WordPerfect was one of the first word-processing programs to hit the market; and many companies were anxious to get their employees up and running on PCs. WordPerfect for DOS had its own protocol; for example, to print a document, you had to hold down the Shift key and simultaneously hit the F7 key on your computer. At first, most users had a "cheat sheet" taped to the top of their keyboard. But after a while, an avid user would begin to memorize certain keystrokes and become very proficient at using the software. As new versions of word-processing programs became available, users would purchase WordPerfect because of their acquired expertise. It would have been extremely costly and inefficient to buy another word-processing program and start again from scratch. In a sense, buyers became captive to WordPerfect. As new versions came out, users had no other choice than to buy WordPerfect. Once an employee was trained in a particular software program, the cost of switching to another was prohibitive. Clearly, aggressiveness paid off for WordPerfect. The power of switching costs kept WordPerfect at the top of the market until it was dethroned by a major discontinuity—the change from a DOS-based environment to a Windows-based environment.

Controlling scarce resources. If a company is aggressive in an industry that requires certain scarce resources to offer a specific product, the first mover can take control of the scarce resource. Basically, if you control the supply of raw materials for an industry, you control the industry. DeBeers aggressively acquired diamond mines and today owns about 80 percent of the diamond mines in the world. Rubies and emeralds are far more rare, but DeBeers restricts the flow of diamonds mined every year to artificially make them a more precious gemstone than they should be. Bottom line: if you control the raw material, you control the market.

Risks of Being Aggressive

Despite the obvious benefits associated with aggressiveness in seeking new growth opportunities, there are also numerous risks—specifically, three major risks are explained in the following paragraphs.

Capital investment. If a company takes an aggressive stance in developing a new product or service, there are never any guarantees. Letting someone else stick out his or her neck to test the waters can be a big advantage. Why not let someone verify if the new product idea is good, making it safer to invest? Bowman Corporation invested a significant amount of resources to initiate development of the pocket calculator. Texas Instruments subsequently used Bowman's findings as a platform to become the dominant player in the market.

Imitation. Another risk associated with being aggressive is the possibility that competitors ride free on your R&D investment. You spend millions of dollars developing a new product or a new way to offer a service, and someone else comes along and copies what you do. It happens all the time. If you think you can protect a new product with a patent, you may be fooling yourself. Patents are extremely effective with simple technologies (e.g., Velcro) and with pharmaceuticals. Unfortunately, with most products competitors can work their way around a patent to develop a competing product.

Competence-destroying change. The biggest downside to taking an aggressive stance is the threat of a competence-destroying change. A competence-destroying change is so influential that it completely replaces the need for your product. A classical example of a company that proactively invested millions of dollars in R&D only to see another product replace it is the Sony Beta machine. Within a short period of time, VHS technology had replaced demand for Sony's Betamax.

To Be or Not to Be?

Reviews seem to be mixed whether aggressive or passive is better. Recall that I performed a comprehensive study of approximately 200 companies and tested the simultaneous impact of:

- Market factors

- Leadership and capabilities

- Strategies

Even though all three areas were simultaneously important, the single biggest predictor of growth was a variable I called "strategic aggressiveness." Although aggressiveness has its risks, quite often the decision not to decide has even more risk. Some companies have been successful using a passive approach, but proacting pays off better than reacting most of the time—aggressiveness puts you right in the middle of the game, passiveness keeps you on the sidelines. You will never sustain leap growth by sitting on the sidelines.

Know When to Hold 'em, Know When to Fold 'em

Value innovation is exciting. It's a chance to let your creative juices flow. Even with a lot of risk associated with sticking your neck out and trying to come up with something new, the payoffs are huge. But let's face it, most of the time new product introductions fail. According to Group EFO, a Connecticut-based consulting firm that annually surveys new-product managers at major companies, only 42 percent of the products that hit the market each year live up to the expectations of those managing the products; and if we consider medium-sized and smaller companies, the failure rate becomes even larger.

Many executives believe the biggest risks revolve around developing dogs instead of winners, but many failures result from hanging onto a project too long—trying to reach perfection when perfection isn't required. Many times, the window of opportunity presents itself very quickly, and if your business isn't ready to react, someone else will seize the day.

Tom Peters, well-known author and consultant, points out that "life is [simply] a series of approximations." In a recent issue of *Fast Company*, Peters discusses the essence of "Wow Projects," stating that managers never get a project right the first time— never! Holding onto something until it's nearly perfect is a sure-fire way to kill its potential. Continually tweaking a value innovation until it's "just right" may not only cause your business to miss a growth opportunity but may allow a competitor to beat you to the chase. Growth champions react quickly. They create or respond to opportunities and hit the market as soon as possible rather than sitting in the laboratory making incremental improvements that customers would never notice anyway!

Consider a company like IDEO. IDEO is one of the most innovative product design companies in the world, winning more Industrial Design Excellence Awards than any other company in the last ten years. Not only does the company continuously develop value innovations (over 4,000 new products and services since its inception in 1978), but it also offers strategic services and "boot camps" to help other companies become innovative. To this end, David Kelley, CEO of IDEO, reminds us that to be successful we must "fail often to succeed sooner."

What he means is that we must embrace risks, accept failure, and (as Nike so eloquently states) just do it. Many fine opportunities are lost because no one is willing to make the first move, to take the risk, to actually do something instead of just talking about doing it.

You tell yourself, "Sounds great in theory, but how can we make this happen at our company?" To develop a new idea, put it into a prototype, and get the product to market must start with good communication. At Hewlett-Packard, for example, Ned Barnholt, senior vice president, says that one of the key attributes that allows H-P to be so successful in introducing new products is the synergy between research, product development, and marketing. Most of the product development occurs in H-P's business organizations, whereas the majority of research is done in a laboratory setting. Each group leverages the other to produce a steady stream of new products.

Endnotes

1. W. Chan Kim and Renee Mauborgne, "Strategy, Value Innovation, and the Knowledge Economy," *Sloan Management Review* 40, no. 3 (Spring 1999): 41–54.

2. W. Chan Kim and Renee Mauborgne, "Value Innovation: The Strategic Logic of High Growth," *Harvard Business Review* (January-February 1997): 103–12.

7

Making New Friends

Relationship Strategies for Growth

*B*y now you should have a pretty good understanding of your market drivers and how effectively your business can incorporate these drivers. Maybe you have even identified some growth opportunities that you want to pursue. You ask yourself, "Are we ready? Are all our ducks in a row or do we even have the right ducks?"

Understandably, many business executives become very excited about the pursuit of growth opportunities. They spend considerable resources to understand their markets and even more resources trying to ramp up their businesses to exploit these opportunities. Then when the big day comes—the day they decide to set off on this exciting journey—they hit a wall. "How do we do it?" they ask. "What is our first step? Do we have sufficient resources to pursue this opportunity? If not, what do we still need? How do we get these resources? What are the risks involved? Plain and simple, how do we make it happen?"

These are important questions, and you should think long and hard about each one. Even if you find a great growth opportunity, you may fail miserably if your business is not in a position to exploit the opportunity. Developing effective long-term relationships is one of the most critical skills a growth champion can possess, but surprisingly little has been written on the topic. Relationship strategies come in a variety of choices, and it's important to understand the pluses and minuses of each as well as the factors that determine which strategy is most appropriate for a given situation.

For the remainder of the book, I stress *balance* at many different levels. In Chapter 1, I discussed balance as critical to sustainable, value-driven growth. In this chapter, I focus on the balance between resources and capabilities. Recall from Chapter 4 that resources can be tangible (e.g., a superior product) and intangible (e.g., brand-name recognition, creativity, or technological expertise). Capabilities are skill sets (e.g., systems, leadership, abilities). Growth champions are very astute at achieving a balance between resources and capabilities because they are aware of the options they have to achieve this balance.

Choice of Relationship Strategies

To maintain a proper balance between resources and capabilities, growth companies have three choices: (1) internal development (starting from scratch by doing it on their own); (2) strategic alliances (partnering with another firm); or (3) acquisitions (buying another firm outright). Each of these relationship strategies has distinct advantages and disadvantages. An effective manager has to become familiar with all three choices as well as with the factors that determine which relationship strategy is most appropriate in the given situation. To simply define each of the three relationship strategies and provide a few examples wouldn't be enough. To be effective, you must also know the contingent factors that dictate the appropriateness of each strategy. Therefore, I start with a discussion of choosing between internal development, strategic alliances, or acquisitions. Then I examine what each of these strategies requires to succeed, so by the end of the chapter you should have a pretty good idea of which strategy is most appropriate for a given situation.

Internal-Development Strategies

Assume you are ready to pursue a growth opportunity. The first choice you have is to employ an internal-development strategy—pursuing a growth opportunity by yourself. You don't have to partner with someone else and you don't have to acquire another company. Instead, you do everything on your own—and I mean everything. For example, if you want to expand into a new growth market on your own, you would have to analyze the market; develop manufacturing and/or service products; figure out a way to offer your product or service; purchase the necessary resources; hire, train, and develop new employees; market the new product or service; and finance everything. Although this sounds like a lot of work—and it is—internal development has a lot of advantages.

Internal development is an effective growth strategy—some of the time. Most growth champions are excellent at doing it on their own. Companies like Hewlett-Packard and 3M successfully implement internal-development strategies over and over. Almost every growth company begins with internal development. Odds are that you have already done it. As the company grows in size and acquires more assets, it may consider a joint venture or acquisition. But, initially, most companies begin with internal development.

Unfortunately, many internal-development strategies fall short. What determines if a company can pull off an internal-development strategy? To reduce the risk of failure, it's important to understand common problems associated with internal development. Four shortcomings are associated with internal development as seen in Figure 7.1.[1]

FIGURE 7.1   Challenges Associated with Internal Development

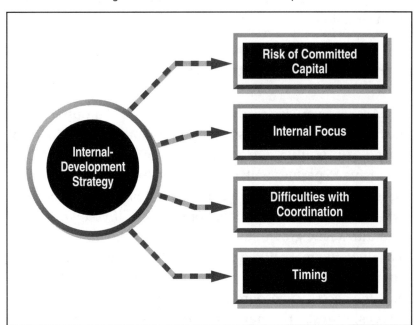

Risk of committed capital. Numerous studies and count-less companies have shown that large-scale entry into a growth opportunity using internal development dramatically improves the success rate for a business. Although large-scale entry creates better long-term returns compared to small-scale entry, it also ex-poses a business to considerable short-term risks. Large-scale en-try may cause a significant drain on cash flow, and it may be detrimental to profit in the short run. Therefore, many com-panies tend to hedge by scaling back their entry into an industry from fear of investing significant resources. Many times when this happens, the business fails to commit sufficient resources and the entire venture fails. So before you decide to embark on an internal development strategy, know what the costs are to in-vest aggressively enough to make the project successful.

Internal focus. It is quite common for an executive to get caught up in a focus on internal attributes of the company rather than on drivers in the market. This often happens when companies try to follow the 3M model—basically, let your research scientists go "wild." Most don't realize that 3M has a very good pulse on market drivers and tries to create technologies to meet those drivers. What many companies try to do when pursuing internal development as a means to grow is to let their researchers do what they know how to do best—create new technologies. Although these new technologies may be intriguing to research scientists, most of the time the market places no value on their activities.

I have had numerous encounters with high-tech research engineers trying to advance knowledge in their specific areas. I was recently consulting with a group of engineers who studies the impact of different materials to improve the efficiency and power generation of gas and diesel engines. Their research facility has been identified as one of the leading materials research centers in the world. The engineers do an outstanding job of pioneering new technologies, but over the years they have learned that breakthrough technologies don't always translate into good business decisions. Historically, this group has devoted considerable efforts *internally* to develop new technologies. By pursuing internal development, however, the researchers put all of their resources into developing a given technology rather than trying to commercialize it. A company often becomes enamored with a new development; instead of thinking about external-growth opportunities, it focuses on internal activities.

It seems as though many companies use internal-development strategies when they create new technologies. To overcome the problem of internal focus, there should be a tight link between engineering and marketing, which will help to alleviate problems associated with focusing exclusively on technology and ignoring value creation.

Difficulties with coordination. Of the three relationship strategies, internal development provides the biggest challenge in terms of internal coordination. It stresses the internal infrastructure of a company more than a joint venture or acquisition. First, if a company tries to pursue numerous internal-development ventures at once, it can have a significant drain on cash flow. Dead-end projects may drain capital away from promising projects. In addition, a manager will often overestimate synergies when trying to coordinate a new venture. "We already have a great manufacturing process in place. Now we can use the same process for this new venture." Or "We already have a great distribution network in place. I'm sure our distributors will support our new venture." Sometimes the best intentions are only that—intentions. Managers will often optimistically assume that they can capitalize on other activities in the company to assist in the development of a new venture, only to find that they have overestimated possible synergies. Maybe you have some synergies that you can exploit for your business. Great, but just be careful that you don't lose touch with reality and find out too late that you talked yourself into a new venture that was destined to fail. Bottom line: trying to coordinate all of the diverse functional activities involved in pursuing internal development may create numerous headaches for the person in charge.

Timing. Successful implementation of an internal-development strategy may take years before a product gets to market. Then count on additional time before the company begins to realize a profit. One good way to overcome problems with timing issues is to establish project teams so that workers in different functional areas can concentrate on specific tasks at the same time. For example, as manufacturing is working on a way to produce a new product, marketing can be working on increasing demand and human resources can be ramping up sufficient personnel.

Why pursue an internal-development strategy when there are so many risks involved? The choice to pursue an opportunity using an internal-development strategy has a big benefit— you don't have to share. As kids, sharing becomes ingrained as something good, the right thing to do. Now that you're an adult, sharing is *not* always good. If your business has distinctive competencies and you have the skills to exploit it on your own, then do it. It won't be easy, but in the long run (and remember, we are concerned about the long run), you will realize much more benefit than sharing your competencies with a partner. Some factors to consider for effective use of internal development are:

Don't	Do
Focus on technology advancement	Focus on value innovation
Overestimate synergies	Set realistic expectations
Underestimate difficulties with coordination	Carefully estimate timing/ cost
Conservatively scale back	Invest sufficient resources for success
Share distinctive competencies	Use capabilities to exploit resources

Starbucks is a fine example of a company that has effectively used internal development to grow. During 1999, Starbucks opened an average of one store a day in the United States and Canada. In 1987, the Seattle-based company had a mere 17 stores. In 1996, the company surpassed the 1,000-store mark. CEO Howard Schultz has effectively grown his company on his own—without sharing the benefits of the Starbucks name with others. He states, "Over the short term, franchising Starbucks would drive up revenues. But over the long term, it would be a giant mistake." Today, Starbucks has over 2,000 locations. Why has internal development been so successful for Starbucks? The company has a very strong brand name and the coffee market is mature. As Starbucks expands internationally, the company will no longer be able to do it on their own. To gain access to some foreign markets, the only choice a company has is to enter into a joint venture or some other strategic alliance.

Strategic-Alliance Strategies

What if you don't have the skills to do it on your own? Or what if the market dictates that you need to exploit an opportunity now or forever hold your peace? If your business faces either of these scenarios, then some form of strategic alliance may be necessary. While it may be a tough call, sometimes it's better to give up some of the kitty rather than lose the whole jackpot.

Often a company can't pursue growth on its own. While it may have some resource, let's say a new product, it may not possess the skills and capabilities to exploit the resource. Or it may take several years to ramp up to get a product to market—unfortunately, the opportunity to grow is here today and will be gone tomorrow. In these cases a strategic alliance makes a lot of sense. Each partner has something of value to bring to the table, yet each partner cannot do it alone. Noel Forgeard, CEO of Airbus Industries (an alliance made up of British, German, and French companies) is up front about the importance of using strategic alliances effectively. He states, "It is partnerships which have helped create shareholder value. It is obvious that none of the Airbus partners would be able to establish a company on a par with Boeing in a world market by itself." Airbus Industries has been created from a strategic alliance; without the partnership, Airbus would never have existed.

Once an executive decides to enter into a strategic alliance, the next step is to decide which one. Strategic alliances come in many forms. The most common are joint ventures, franchising, and licensing.

Joint ventures. A joint venture, in and of itself, can take on many shapes. All joint ventures involve an agreement between two or more companies to form some type of partnership. In an ideal joint venture, each party has some needs and the other partners possess the missing links. I often hear executives refer to joint ventures as marriages, so to get value out of the relationship, all parties have to bring something to the dance.

It's common to see joint ventures in rapidly evolving industries. When changes take place quickly, it's difficult to keep up with the Joneses. Businesses don't have the luxury of developing new technologies in-house; instead, they must respond quickly to changes in the environment. And they do it through effective use of a joint venture strategy. In industries like pharmaceuticals, biotechnology, software development, and telecommunications, companies partner with each other simply to try to keep pace. It's not uncommon in these types of industries to actually see companies partner with their competitors. What was unheard of a few years ago now happens on a daily basis. To keep pace, the issue is not whether a company should enter into an alliance, it's who should our partner be?

Findings from a recent study performed by Andersen Consulting indicate that joint venture alliances will create upwards of $40 trillion within the next few years. While the use of joint ventures is increasing at a rapid rate, the study found that 61 percent of corporate partnerships are not successful. Pam Moret, vice president of variable assets at American Express Financial Advisors, says that the traditional build-or-buy decision has taken on a third option: to bond.[2]

One difficulty with joint ventures is developing metrics that truly measure whether the venture has succeeded or failed. Hewlett-Packard has put the proverbial "money where its mouth is." H-P recently entered into a joint venture with Telecom and Qwest Communications International, an Internet service provider. There will be no question whether this venture has succeeded. If the partnership makes money, then H-P gets paid. If the partnership doesn't make money, H-P receives nothing. Rather than selling $500 million of server hardware, software, and services to Qwest, H-P has provided everything free. The companies have created a new business called CyberCenters that offers a full spectrum of Internet solutions, 24/7. H-P's chief marketing officer, Nick Earle, notes that "this is a pretty significant change in alliances. Most people [only] talk about partnerships, but in this partnership, we're only paid if we make money."

Franchising. Like any strategic-alliance strategy, franchising too comes in many different forms. Regardless of the form, however, franchising can allow for significant growth in a short period with relatively low short-term financial risk. Numerous studies have shown that service businesses are more likely to use franchising than manufacturing firms. Also, franchising is more popular with smaller firms than larger firms, given the low level of seed money needed to successfully franchise. A company choosing to franchise to achieve fast growth enters into a contractual agreement for a specific geographic region. The franchiser receives an initial investment and royalties, and the franchisee receives the rights to offer a specific product or service, using the expertise, brand name, distribution channels, training, and support from the franchiser.

Is franchising an effective growth strategy under the right conditions? I think that SUBWAY would say so. The first SUBWAY sandwich franchise opened in Wallingford, Connecticut in 1974. A decade later, the first international SUBWAY restaurant opened its doors in Bahrain. In August 1995, the SUBWAY chain celebrated 30 years of success and witnessed the opening of their 11,000th restaurant. In the past ten years, SUBWAY has grown consistently and sustainably from 2,888 stores to 13,600 stores.

Licensing. Another strategic alliance strategy is licensing. With this strategy, a licensing arrangement is made in which one company is allowed to manufacture a product or offer a service using another company's products, brand name, or technological know-how. Franchising is popular among smaller firms, whereas licensing is used by companies of all sizes. Many companies use licensing as a means of growth. Coca-Cola and Harley-Davidson have been very effective in generating significant revenue streams by licensing the use of their names. Harley-Davidson has put its name on everything from motorcycle paraphernalia to cigarettes to colognes. In contrast, some companies license their name to impact sales of other products in their portfolio. For example, Caterpillar licenses its name to other manufacturers trying to increase sales of its earthmoving equipment. Caterpillar carefully chooses licensees such as Wolverine (a high-quality boot manufacturer) to produce CAT boots. The boots are manufactured to be durable and rugged in order to portray the types of earthmoving equipment that Caterpillar manufactures. Caterpillar could easily sell its brand to numerous manufacturers to generate greater royalties from licensing. Instead, the company carefully analyzes appropriate products and licensees to improve the management of its brand name in order to excite current and future customers, employees, and investors about the brand instead of licensing to generate royalties.

Difficulties of using strategic-alliance strategies. Whatever approach a company uses to create a strategic alliance, there are usually some problems associated with bringing together the skills and capabilities of two or more businesses. Again, three downsides are associated with strategic alliances, as seen in Figure 7.2.

Sharing profit. The most basic downside to partnering with another firm is that you have to give up a certain percentage of profit. Many companies are willing to forgo some profit by sharing the investment cost with a partner. In a sense, the strategic alliance is a way to hedge against unforeseen risks—if you are

FIGURE 7.2   Challenges Associated with Strategic Alliances

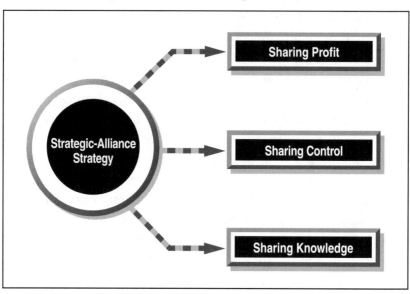

willing to share the risks and development costs with me up front, I will share profits with you down the road.

Sharing control. The second drawback of entering into a strategic alliance is sharing control. This can be particularly detrimental if the partnering companies have differing philosophies. As Jerrold Kaplan, CEO of Go Corporation, stated so eloquently in describing his company's strategic alliance with IBM, "When the elephant dances with the cat, it has to be careful where it steps and the cat has to be nimble."

I have worked with several companies to provide assistance in putting together joint ventures. It surprises me that executives often assume that ownership determines control. For example, if two firms entered into a 50-50 joint venture, everyone assumes that each firm has a 50 percent control in decision making. But ownership doesn't necessarily dictate control. If you enter into a 50-50 joint venture, you can stipulate that even though ownership is evenly shared, you still have majority control in decisions. All you need is an astute attorney to draw up a contract that specifies ownership and control. As long as your partner agrees, it's that easy.

Sharing knowledge. The biggest potential downside to entering into a strategic alliance is sharing critical knowledge with your partner. The average joint venture in the United States lasts a mere three to five years. So what happens when the joint venture dissolves? If you have shared critical trade secrets, your ex-partner may now become your worst enemy. You have trained the partner well, and now he or she knows all of your secrets.

One way to minimize the risk of sharing knowledge is to make your partner dependent on you in some other way. For example, you can become a major supplier or customer to one of your partner's other businesses. That way, if the partner is dependent on you in some other way, he or she would be less likely to try to take advantage by exploiting knowledge that you once shared in a joint venture.

Some benefits to using strategic-alliance strategies. An often overlooked benefit of establishing a strategic alliance is the learning process that your organization can take away from the partnership to use in other areas of business. In the long run, many companies realize benefits from a joint venture partnership long after the partnership has dissolved. In a recent study of almost 900 joint ventures, Harvard Professors Bharat Anand and Tarun Khanna found that certain types of joint ventures provided better learning opportunities than others.[3] They were able to show that joint research and development ventures and joint production ventures created significant learning opportunities for value creation, whereas joint marketing ventures did not. In the same study, it was shown that experience is an important predictor of success or failure in a joint venture. It usually takes about four joint venture partnerships before a company accumulates enough experience to be profitable from an alliance.

Strategic alliances are also an excellent way to gain access to new markets. Consider Texas Instruments (TI). Until recently, TI made heavy use of internal-development strategies, but over the past decade the company has changed its tune, utilizing strategic alliances to pursue growth opportunities. When the semiconductor industry began to specialize, TI began to form a broad web of strategic alliances. By the mid-90s, TI had partnerships ranging from smaller companies like Cyrix to large multinationals like Japan's Canon and Hitachi. These partnerships allow TI to aggressively pursue growth opportunities without having to make huge investments. Even more important, these alliances allow TI to react quickly to take advantage of big opportunities that require fast actions. Have strategic alliances helped TI grow? In the past year, TI realized 11 percent growth in revenues, an astounding 79 percent growth in operating margins, and 83 percent growth in earnings per share.

In summary, some factors to consider for effective use of strategic alliances are:

Don't	Do
Give away unnecessary knowledge	Try to make your partner dependent on you
Give away control	Create a contract to protect yourself
Blindly enter into an alliance	Make sure your partner fulfills a necessary need
Expose yourself to too much risk	Share development costs and risks
Close the books when it's over	Learn from each experience

Acquisition Strategies

A final relationship strategy a company can use to pursue a growth opportunity is acquisition. Rather than trying to do it on your own or partner with another company, an acquisition

FIGURE 7.3   Challenges Associated with Acquisitions

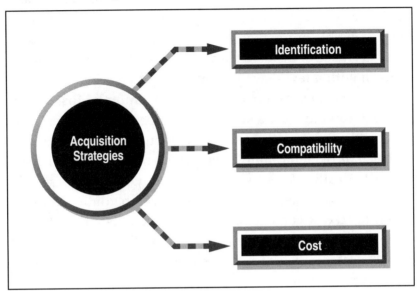

strategy involves the outright purchase of another company. Numerous studies have shown that acquisition strategies are difficult to pull off, and more often than not the acquirer never profits from the acquisition. Figure 7.3 illustrates the three major hurdles a company must overcome to successfully acquire another company.

Identification. One of the most difficult things associated with using this strategic choice is the ability to identify a good acquisition candidate. Many companies try to acquire a top player in another industry. For example, Rubbermaid Inc. states that it will acquire only the number one or number two player in a market. While the upside of acquiring a top player in a new market has the benefit of instantly becoming the market leader, the downside is that most often buying a top player in a market carries a huge sticker price. Basically, if you want the best—today—you will have to pay for it.

Rather than going after the leader in a market, it can be much more profitable if you can identify a struggling firm—and not just any struggling firm but one that has valuable assets (either tangible or intangible) but no management expertise to take advantage of them. Ideally, it's a situation where you could come in with a few management changes and, by using your company's expertise, turn the company around. Most important, you can purchase a struggling company for a lot less than a market leader. The Walt Disney Company is one example. Roy Disney took over the family business as a result of Walt Disney's untimely death. Walt was a visionary, Roy pragmatic, so they balanced each other. When Roy took over, he didn't have the vision to take advantage of Disney's accumulated assets. The company licensed the Disney name rather than keeping such a valuable asset in-house; and management also kept many classic videos stored in a vault.

A lot of outsiders realized the vast gold mine within Disney, but unfortunately, Disney insiders didn't see what outsiders saw. So Disney became a prime acquisition target. Things were looking bleak for the Disney family until they had the foresight to hire Michael Eisner to turn the company around. One of the first things Eisner did when he took over was to double the price of admission tickets to the Disney theme parks; and attendance stayed almost the same. As mentioned earlier, he then decided to release (and even rerelease) many of the videos that had been stored in a vault. He took back the Disney name rather than granting licensing rights that would have allowed others to make money from the Disney name. All of this potential was waiting to be exploited, and many corporate raiders recognized the opportunity—the ideal situation for pursuing an acquisition. Find a company that is being mismanaged, buy it for pennies on the dollar, and then turn it around. A lot easier said than done. It is extremely difficult to find opportunities such as Disney offered. Most acquirers simply identify the market leader and then pounce, never realizing payback or profit from the venture.

Compatibility. Many companies seem to become so enamored with number crunching that they fail to see the big picture when pursuing acquisition targets. They ask: "When can we achieve payback?" or "How does our return on assets (ROA) look?" While these are important issues, they are only part of the equation. Seldom do I run across executives who question the soft side of acquisitions.

What do I mean by the term *soft side*? Rather than focusing exclusively on financials, growth champions also focus on issues such as corporate culture and employee needs. When an acquiring company has a corporate culture distinctly different from the acquiree's, but tries to force its culture on the acquiree, that is usually a surefire way to kill the new venture. Nicholas Teti, president of DuPont Pharmaceutical, says, "Cultural clashes in the megamergers are significant and should never be understated. I've learned the hard way that culture is a palatable, tangible entity. It is not something to be taken lightly."[4]

When Cisco Systems, the worldwide leader in networking for the Internet, goes shopping for a new company, it looks for two things—a good match in technology and a good match in culture.[5] Has Cisco been able to grow through acquisitions? It was growing at a phenomenal rate of about 100 percent a year through 1996. From 1997 through 1999, the company grew at a "modest" rate of 57 percent, reaching annual sales in 1999 of $12.15 billion. By the end of 1999, Cisco had acquired 42 companies and was still counting. Cisco is truly one of today's most effective managers of acquisitions. *Fortune* magazine recently referred to Cisco as an "acquisition engine."[6] Because of Cisco's unique strategy in acquiring other companies, it makes no layoffs, and turnover is virtually nonexistent. Vice President for Business Development Mike Volpi says, "Cisco's [acquisition] strategy can be boiled down to five things. We look at a company's vision; its short-term success with customers; its long-term strategy; the chemistry of the people with ours; and its geographic proximity." Note that all of these issues are soft-side concerns. Admittedly, Cisco does crunch numbers when deciding on an acquisition target, but it is the soft-side issues that make or break a buying decision. While this seems like common sense, consider the high failure rates of acquisitions. Why do so many fail? Because executives focus on numbers rather than soft-side issues.

So how do you size up a company to see if it will fit into your world? Dan Scheinman, Cisco's "culture cop," says there are certain qualities he looks for in an acquisition target to see if it will fit in at Cisco:

- *Consider risk-taking propensity.* Successful companies have to be willing to make a mistake once in a while. If not, they are not daring enough.

- *See if you agree with top management's past decisions.* Scheinman actually role-plays, going over past decisions the company has made to see if they think in similar terms.

- *Be observant in the negotiation process.* You can learn a lot about a potential partner's motives simply by taking note during the negotiation process.

Cost. Of the three relationship strategies, acquisition is the most expensive. Fortunately, there are ways to negotiate the price. Probably one of the best situations to look for, if you are trying to increase your negotiating leverage, is to find a solid company that is feeling some heat to meet short-term cash obligations. If a company has poor liquidity (insufficient cash), quite often the market will undervalue its stock.

It's not surprising that only 23 percent of all acquisitions earn their cost of capital, according to a study performed by a group of consultants at McKinsey that analyzed a group of 116 companies over an 11-year period. Growth companies that successfully use acquisition strategies are usually going after a needed intangible asset that would be difficult to develop internally, such as technological expertise, market access, or brand-name recognition.

In summary, some factors to consider for effective use of acquisitions are:

Don't	Do
Focus exclusively on financials. . . .	Understand the soft side
Automatically go after the market leader	Try to identify undervalued companies
Blindly enter into an alliance.	Make sure your partner fulfills a need
Expose yourself to too much risk	Share development costs and risks

Which One Should I Use?

By now it's obvious that each of the three relationship strategies (internal development, strategic alliances, and acquisitions) has distinct advantages and distinct disadvantages. Therefore, there are appropriate and inappropriate times to use each strategy. To decide which to use in a given context, you must consider the specific situations. I have found four sets of factors that I discuss with my clients as they decide which relationship strategy to use. The factors that commonly come into play when a company tries to pursue a new growth opportunity are: synergistic opportunities, barriers to entry, market timing, and risk. Figure 7.4, summarizes which strategies are usually most appropriate based on these four factors.

Synergistic Opportunities

When a company pursues a new growth opportunity, the new business may be similar to something the company cur-

FIGURE 7.4   Choosing the Best Relationship Strategy

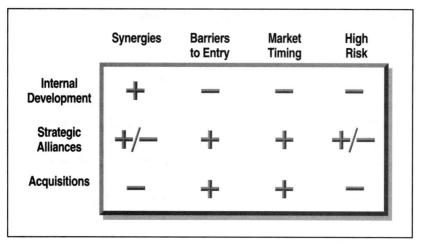

	Synergies	Barriers to Entry	Market Timing	High Risk
Internal Development	+	–	–	–
Strategic Alliances	+/–	+	+	+/–
Acquisitions	–	+	+	–

rently does. The company may already have experience and/or expertise in this new area. The more related the new growth opportunity is to what the company has previously done, the easier it is to take advantage of *synergy*. Synergy is probably one of the most overused terms in industry—and many executives don't even understand its true meaning. Synergy occurs when you can accomplish more by working together than by working individually (e.g., $1 + 1 = 3$). Let me digress for a moment to give you an example of synergy, which may seem a little off-the-wall, but I can guarantee that you will never forget the true meaning of synergy. I use the following example in my executive development courses; years later, I'll run into a former participant who still remembers the example.

There are two types of people in this world—gas-grill people and charcoal-grill people. When I'm cooking outside, I definitely prefer charcoal over gas. Yes, it's more work, but you can't beat the flavor. What's the first thing you do before you light a fire? I know you're already thinking that you "douse the coals with a lot of lighter fluid, yeah, a lot of lighter fluid!" Before you "sparingly" put on lighter fluid, what do you do with the coals?

Have you ever wondered why you stack them in a pyramid before you light them? Because when you stack coals in a pyramid, as one coal gets hot, it spreads to all of the adjacent coals. As the adjacent coals get hot, they spread to other adjacent coals (including the original hot coal) and so on and so on. You get the idea. The individual pieces of coal all feed off of each other and get hotter faster by benefiting from each other—synergy. Can you imagine if you individually placed each coal on a grill, where none of them was physically touching another one and each piece of coal was trying to heat up individually? You would never be able to get them hot (or if you did, your food would have that peculiar taste of lighter fluid we have all experienced at one time or another). So next time you're cooking on a charcoal grill, think about synergy.

OK, now that you have an image of synergy "burned" into your mind, let's get back to business. When pursuing a new growth opportunity that is related to an area of internal expertise for a business, synergy may take on many different forms.

Brand. If a company has a strong brand in one business, it may be able to extend its brand into other businesses. There are numerous examples of companies that have created new growth opportunities by extending their brand into new markets. Earlier in the book, we talked about how Arm & Hammer created new growth opportunities when it was discovered that baking soda absorbed odors. Arm & Hammer was quick in extending its brand name into almost every conceivable product that in some way was related to odor absorption: baking-soda toothpaste, carpet cleaner, body deodorant, and laundry detergent. Many restaurant chains have extended their brand names into new markets. For example, Taco Bell now sells its salsa in grocery stores, creating significant growth in a related market. Even clothes manufacturers are extending their brands into new products. Eddie Bauer and Ford Motor Company joined forces to come up with the Eddie Bauer Ford Explorer. Obviously, there is a lot of growth opportunity in exploiting a successful brand name.

Distribution channels. Another good source of synergistic opportunity is to take advantage of established distribution channels. If a company has strong distribution channels for one product, it may be able to realize additional growth by pursuing new opportunities using those same distribution channels. Numerous companies have achieved significant growth this way. Currently, Amazon.com is attempting to pursue this very strategy. As most of us know, Amazon.com started out selling books on the Internet. If consumers buy books over the Internet, why not try to sell other products? While a person is on Amazon.com looking for a book, they now have the opportunity to buy CDs and DVDs, electronics and software, toys and video games, and home-improvement products. Amazon.com plans to sell an even wider variety of products in the future.

In a similar manner, automobile dealerships have grown into new markets by exploiting their distribution channel. You can walk into a dealership and, while there, can purchase or lease a new vehicle *and* obtain financing all at the same time. Similarly, in the past when you walked into almost any bank, you could deposit or withdraw money, take out a loan, or buy a T-bill. After significant deregulation in 1987, banks were allowed to sell other financial products. Because they had such a strong distribution network already, they figured out that if a customer stops in to make a financial transaction, why not offer other financial products? Now you can walk into a bank and in addition to buying all of its traditional financial products, you can buy stocks, bonds, mutual funds, and even life insurance.

Manufacturing processes and raw materials. An often over-looked source of synergy is expertise in manufacturing and raw materials. Exploiting synergistic opportunities in manufacturing and raw materials usage can create tremendous growth opportunities. Rubbermaid Inc. offers a great example of a company that has created new growth opportunities by exploiting the manufacturing expertise that it developed for different uses of its raw materials—polymers and plastics. While Rubbermaid may seem like a company in totally unrelated products that range from storage devices and kitchen products to garbage cans, all of its diversification efforts share one thing in common—materials. By exploiting its expertise in polymers and plastics, Rubbermaid has realized significant growth opportunities in new product expansion.

If a company is trying to take advantage of synergy, internal development usually tends to be the most appropriate strategy. As long as you have the resources and capabilities to grow on your own, it doesn't make a lot of sense to enter into a joint venture or make an acquisition.

Barriers to Entry

The second contingency factor that will help determine which of the three relationship strategies is most appropriate is barriers to entry—that is, factors that make it difficult for a new firm to enter an industry. Barriers to entry can vary from strong brand-name recognition to scale efficiencies gained by producing large quantities of a product at lower cost. For example, it would be very difficult for a new company to enter into the cola industry, given strong brands such as Coca-Cola and Pepsi. Not only would a new entrant have to invest in advertising to make consumers aware of a new brand, but they would somehow have to lure customers away from a soft drink that they may be very loyal to. Similarly, it would be very difficult for a new player to enter into the airplane manufacturing industry. Boeing recently acquired McDonnell Douglas to become the largest airplane manufacturer in the world. Boeing has billions of dollars in assets. It would be virtually impossible for a new player to enter the industry, simply because the capital requirements are prohibitive.

So if entry barriers are high, it would be extremely difficult (and inadvisable) to pursue growth via an internal development strategy. Most successful growth companies realize the difficulties of overcoming significant barriers to entry. Rather than trying to do it on their own, many growth champions will attempt to partner with a firm already in the industry.

Acquisition strategies are a common way to overcome entry barriers. To pursue its globalization growth initiative, GE has effectively used several acquisition strategies to overcome difficulties in gaining access to specific Japanese markets. Recently, GE acquired the business infrastructure and salesforce of Toho Mutual Life to become competitive in the Japanese insurance industry. For similar reasons, GE recently acquired the consumer loan business of Japan's Lake Corporation to add to its consumer finance business in Japan. Jack Welch, CEO of GE, recently stated, "Our Japanese [acquisition] initiatives are part of a multiyear focus on globalization that produced $43 billion in 1998 and a growth rate for GE outside the United States that has been double our U.S. growth rate for ten years." To attempt to overcome entry barriers associated with gaining access to these markets via internal development would be virtually impossible.

Market Timing

It is often critical to jump on a market opportunity quickly, whereas at other times a company has a growth opportunity and the luxury to cultivate its capabilities over many years before others even realize an opportunity exists. If timing is critical, internal development is usually not the best choice. Effective internal development may take many years before the product or service hits the market. On the other hand, a joint venture strategy may only take a year or two until new products or services hit the market. Acquisitions are the quickest of all. The day an acquisition takes place, the acquirer has access to new markets. So market timing can be critical in selecting an appropriate relationship strategy.

Netscape has effectively managed to keep pace in an industry that literally evolves at e-speed. Given that market timing is so critical in the Internet's evolution, it is extremely difficult for companies to grow by using internal development as a strategic choice. Netscape has developed Navigator and Communicator by partnering with numerous organizations; and by 1997 was outsourcing to almost 40,000 developers to write the Netscape platform. As Netscape has had to rely on numerous strategic alliances, the company is now trying to make a concerted effort to improve the management of its alliances.

Risk

A final factor to consider when trying to decide on a relationship strategy is risk, which is usually associated with financial investment. Simply stated, the more a company invests, the larger the risk exposure. When this is the case, a strategic alliance strategy is usually most appropriate. Many companies enter into joint ventures exclusively because they want to share the risk of start-up costs with a partner rather than absorbing all of the risk themselves.

However, if a company has developed a strong reputation (e.g., quality products and services), risk may be defined as putting the company's reputation in jeopardy. When defining risk in this way, keeping activities in-house will provide better protection of a strong reputation as opposed to sharing decision-making control in a joint venture. So risk is an important contingency factor, but it can be defined in numerous ways, each influencing which relationship strategy will be most appropriate.

Each of these four factors—synergistic opportunities, barriers to entry, market timing, and risk—help us to determine which relationship strategy is most appropriate. Figure 7.4 summarizes when to use and when not to use a particular relationship strategy.

The Art of Balancing Resources and Capabilities

Clearly, if you take each of these contingency factors (synergistic opportunities, entry barriers, market timing, and risk) individually, it may become clear which strategy to use. Unfortunately, life is not that easy. You will have to consider all of these factors at the same time. Some may point toward one relationship strategy and others toward a different one. When some companies have had past success with a particular relationship strategy, let's say joint ventures, they tend to migrate toward joint ventures all of the time—even when another relationship strategy is more appropriate. Growth champions, however, realize that different situations dictate different growth strategies. They don't commit to a particular strategic choice.

Nestlé has achieved 70 percent of its growth via acquisitions in the 1990s to enter mature markets. Through these acquisitions, Nestlé has developed new proprietary expertise in product development, distribution channels, and an organizational structure that allows rapid dissemination of new ideas, resulting in synergistic opportunities. So how will Nestlé respond? Rather than continuing use of acquisitions, Nestlé plans to achieve 70 percent of its growth over the next decade via internal development. It is letting the situation dictate the best relationship strategy, which is typical of most growth champions.

Now consider an example of a company that had tremendous growth opportunity but failed to choose the most appropriate relationship strategy for its situation. Have you ever heard of EMI, Ltd.? You probably haven't. EMI is the company that invented the CT scanner (catscan machine). Industry experts touted the machine as the greatest advancement in the medical industry since the development of penicillin. In fact, the EMI research engineer who invented the CT scanner won a Nobel prize for his work. EMI had a tremendous growth opportunity; not only did the company have the best product in a high-demand market, but it had the only product. Unfortunately, it didn't have the capabilities (manufacturing, service, and support staff) to exploit this resource. EMI tried to use an internal development strategy to overcome all of its deficiencies. Unfortunately, the product that EMI developed was so outstanding that the market demanded CT scanners immediately—market timing was critical (which you now know means that internal development is not a good strategic choice). Well, along came General Electric with sophisticated manufacturing processes and a sizable salesforce. GE purchased a CT scanner, reverse engineered it, and worked its way around EMI's patent. It manufactured a modified version of EMI's machine, and GE eventually realized the most growth from the CT scanner. What do you think would have happened if EMI had initially approached GE to enter into a joint venture? I would imagine that GE would have jumped at the opportunity, not knowing (at that time) that its engineers would be able to reverse engineer the machine and build a modified version to avoid infringing the patent. If EMI had pursued a strategic alliance rather than trying to do it on its own, the company would have realized significant growth and profit. Instead, the company gave away the farm. That's how critical choosing the most appropriate relationship strategy can be.

Endnotes

1. Charles Hill and Gareth Jones, *Strategic Management: An Integrated Approach,* 2d ed. (Dallas: Houghton Mifflin, 1992).

2. Debra Sparks, "Partners," *Business Week* (October 25, 1999): 106–11.

3. Bharat N. Anand and Tarun Khanna, "Do Firms Learn to Create Value? The Case of Alliances," *Strategic Management Journal* 21 (March 2000): 295–315.

4. Wayne Koberstein, "Sized to Grow," *Pharmaceutical Executive* (February 1999): 40–50.

5. Ronald Henkoff, "Growing Your Company: Five Ways of Doing It Right!" *Fortune* (November 25, 1996): 78–85.

6. Henry Goldblatt, "Cisco's Secret," *Fortune* 140 (9), 1999, 177+.

FOUR

Completing the Puzzle

Creating a Balanced Plan of Attack for Growth

*T*he one common theme that has consistently appeared throughout this book has been balance. If a company can maintain balance, growth will provide numerous rewards; however, when a company loses balance, growth can put a company out of business. This section starts with a discussion of the warning signs associated with unbalanced growth. Effective managers heed the warning signs, but ineffective managers ignore the warning signs and continue full steam ahead.

I discuss, in detail, issues of balance that relate to attaining growth and issues of balance that relate to sustaining growth. Then specific tools are presented to assist managers in putting together a winning action plan to pursue fast growth. You will see how growth champions pursue growth one step at a time. Attaining and sustaining growth is not a matter of making huge jumps; rather, it is the accumulation of many small steps. Small steps allow flexibility and adaptability.

Growing Pains
When Good Growth Turns Bad

*H*ere it is, 8:00 AM Monday morning and time for another board meeting. Everyone slowly shuffles into the boardroom. They sit down despondently. Frustrated and confused, the CEO mutters, "How could this happen? Last year we set out to grow at 30 percent and we exceeded that goal. We are now the number one player in the market. So why aren't we making any money? I don't get it!" She desperately turns to anyone in the room to provide the answer. Everyone is looking down at the table to avoid eye contact—they are silent. No one has an answer.

The exact thing the company was striving for—fast growth —has now unleashed its fury, and the company is experiencing severe growing pains. Customers can't get what they want. Services start sagging. Orders are backlogged. Quality starts to suffer. Worst of all, once the word hits the street, the company has to start worrying about damage control. Unfortunately, management doesn't have time for damage control and problems escalate. In the blink of an eye the company is history.

It's a scene none of us ever wants to be in. Unfortunately, this scenario is more common than you think. Even many of today's growth champions have suffered the strains of too much growth. In a recent article in *Executive Excellence,* Michael Dell admits:

> There is a level of growth that is not only too fast but dangerous and deadly. We [Dell Computer Corporation] grew in one year from $890 million in sales to $2.1 billion in sales. It was exciting, but one year later we hit the wall. We had to learn how to understand the profitability of different parts of our business, where our business was succeeding and where it wasn't, and how to anticipate and build an infrastructure for growth.

Companies experiencing fast growth expose themselves to new risks and new problems. So why on earth are so many companies striving for growth? The good news is that they don't have to be overwhelmed. If management is proactive and comes up with a balanced plan of attack (discussed in the next chapter), many of these problems can be alleviated. Growth champions usually plan for growth before growth happens. Moreover, these plans are flexible, as forecasting fast growth is an inexact science.

Growth's Fury: Feeling the Heat

Many managers pursuing growth become single-minded, too focused. They become so obsessed with growing their business that they take on additional business simply because it's there. They plead, "How can we turn down business if the customers are waiting in line outside our door?" They stop minding the store and don't think about controlling growth. Or maybe they assume someone else is ramping up operations to manage the growth. In either case, they are setting themselves up for a lot of problems. They grow for the sake of growth, not for the sake of value. They become subservient to growth. This is when good growth turns bad.

The CEO finds himself increasingly busy putting out day-to-day fires, inundated by emergencies with no time to step back and see the big picture—what he *should* be doing. The company starts to lose focus. It falls into a cost-cutting mentality. External framing is put on the back burner while the company tries to fig-ure out how to control this monster it has created.

Even though many large companies feel the heat when they let growth get out of control, small companies often feel it even more. Kenneth Gibble, president of Gibble Norden Cham-pion Consulting Engineers, a small 15-person engineering firm on the East Coast, believes that it is critical for small companies to make the initial investment in ramping up operations *before* they take on additional business. He states, "Sometimes it feels like it's a question of what is going to choke you first. Is it the lack of working capital, is it the lack of experienced project man-agers, is it the limited time available to the principal, or is it the inability to hire [employees]."[1] Growing pains can make life really miserable for managers of large companies, but they can usually rebound. Growing pains can put small companies out of business.

Growth requires a lot of commitment—not only to effort but to capital as well. Growth can be expensive. Being overly aggressive in pursuing growth is similar to the couple that buys a new house they can't afford. "Nice house," you think to your-self as you walk up the front steps with your housewarming gift. But when you walk into the house you notice it is empty—no furniture. The proud new homeowners say, "This house is stretching us a little bit for the moment, but we're saving up to buy some furniture." When you visit them a year later, still no furniture. After a few years of living in an empty house that they really couldn't afford in the first place, the couple ends up sell-ing their dream home. They have simply overextended them-

FIGURE 8.1   Five Drivers of Functional Growing Pains

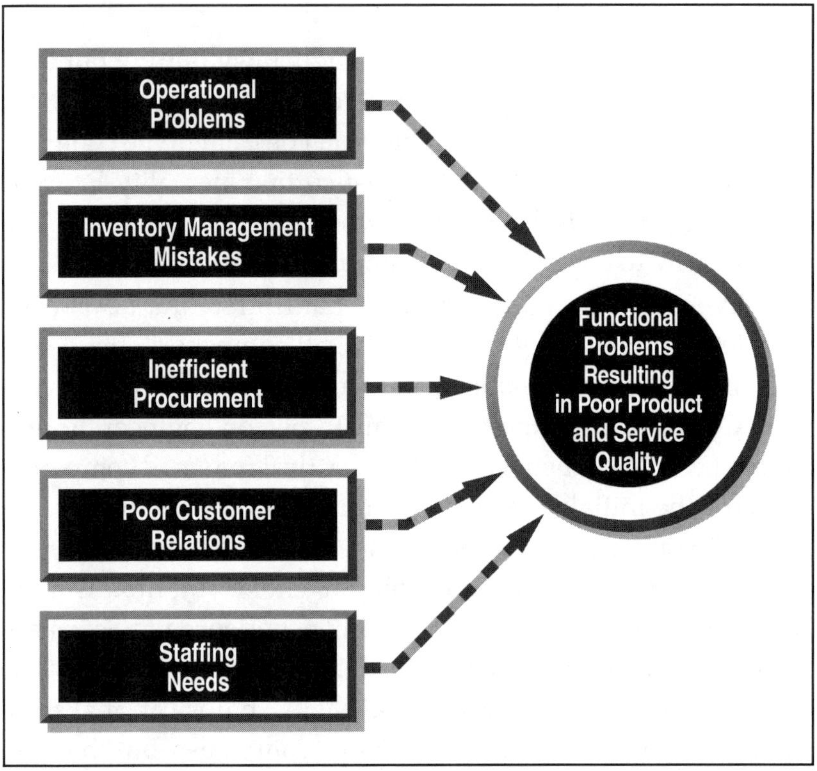

selves, hoping that somehow they could make ends meet. Have you ever known anyone in that situation? Have you ever known any business in that situation?

Knowing the Warning Signs

How can a company avoid overextending itself? How quickly can good growth turn bad? If growth happens when preparedness meets opportunities, how do we know we are prepared? Most important, what do the warning signs look like?

It is critical for managers of fast-growth companies to understand the warning signs of growing pains. Warning signs

FIGURE 8.2 Three Drivers of Integration Growing Pains

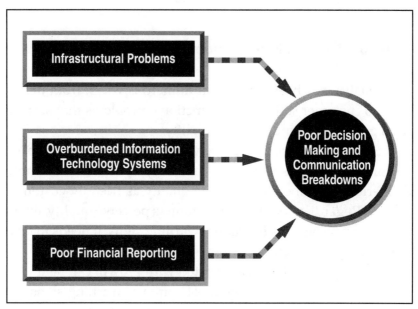

may be a manager's first indication that a business is growing too fast. As warning signs arise, growth champions take immediate action; however, many companies choose to ignore these factors, often resulting in failure of the business.

Even more important, the better management understands these warning signs, the better equipped it will be to proactively *avoid* growing pains. Common warning signs for a company losing the war to growth can be broken down into two distinct categories: functional warning signs and integration warning signs. *Functional warning signs* appear as the result of breakdowns from too much pressure on an individual group within an organization (as presented in Figure 8.1). They usually result in poor product and service quality as seen by customers. *Integration warning signs,* on the other hand, may not be specific to a single group but rather are organizationwide issues that surface as the result of too much growth too fast (as presented in Figure

8.2). Integration warning signs usually result in communication breakdowns and poor decision making.

Functional Issues: Poor Product and Service Quality

Quality has been defined in numerous ways, from defect rates to customer satisfaction. Functional problems that surface from growth ultimately impact quality.

Some customers may perceive quality in terms of product performance, others in terms of accuracy of orders and timely deliveries. Still others may define quality as friendly customer service. Regardless of the way customers perceive quality, when a company recognizes functional warning signs, it needs to take immediate action before customers become dissatisfied.

Functional problems associated with growth can be traced to a specific department. The most common warning signs are usually visible in operations, inventory management, procurement, customer relations, and staffing.

Operational problems. The operations function is probably the most visible area to show signs of stress. A casual stroll through the operating facilities of a company that is unsuccessfully trying to cope with fast growth will show numerous warning signs:

- Shelves crammed with inventory and straining under the weight

- Endless piles and stacks of miscellaneous raw material

- Inventories of work-in-process and finished goods mixed together

- Unopened crates that have been sitting for days

Everyone is so busy trying to keep up with demand that no one has time to do the housekeeping.

New high-tech production systems that were supposed to be used to help manage growth are slowly abandoned. Instead, workers fall back into familiar ways of doing things just to keep their heads above water. The company throws more people on the assembly line, hoping that will be a quick fix. But it's only a band-aid approach. While it stops the bleeding momentarily, soon the situation will take a turn for the worse. Efficiencies are lost and so are cost controls.

Moreover, everyone starts doing their own thing, trying to keep from being a bottleneck at all costs. As numerous modifications are made to handle the increasing pressures of demand (usually through a short-term fix just to make it until tomorrow), operational systems become less and less connected. There is a significant lack of coordination in the operations function. Eventually, operations become highly complex.

Ironically, manufacturers that pursue world-class operations facilities strive for simplicity; many times, fast-growth companies realize this out of necessity. In the early 1990s, General Electric's Multilin plant in Markham, Ontario, a unit of GE's power management group, was suffering significant problems as a result of fast growth. Operations Manager Dan McDonnell recalls, "We'd been growing 30 percent to 40 percent a year—and the wheels were coming off."[2] Operations systems that had worked in the past were now constraining growth. Systems were overburdened and traditional processes were holding back growth.

In response to problems associated with fast growth, the Markham plant decided that simplicity would become a top priority. Management developed flow charts and critically evaluated facility layout maps. McDonnell explains:

We tried to simplify our [manufacturing] organization structure by moving to a focus-factory approach. We broke the organization into smaller chunks, based on product families. We created cross-functional teams and gave them full accountability for managing individual product families.[3]

To redesign production facilities, the company had to completely abandon traditional ways of doing things. The old production mentality had been effective in the past, but as the company started to experience fast growth, complexities that could be tolerated in a slow-growth environment had to be eliminated. McDonnell continues:

> In the past every single product had to be routed through every department, so the shop-floor controls that were needed were enormous—just to track products through the process. And our WIP [work-in-process] inventory was high. But by containing the processes with smaller focus-factory areas, we were able to reduce WIP by 90 percent—and the investment we'd made in shop-floor controls and tracking systems became irrelevant.[4]

The group primarily manufactures protective relay and control devices for power systems. During periods of fast growth, the operations facilities typically had about 600 units scattered throughout the facility in various stages of manufacturing at any given time. After the plant was able to simplify what was once a highly complex environment, the group was able to have as few as 12 units in production at a time, while still able to meet the demands of fast growth.

Inventory management mistakes. Problems in inventory management are also quite common in companies trying to keep pace with fast growth. Managers desperately try to determine inventory levels, safety stock, and "stock-outs." Because inventory cycle times decrease during periods of fast growth, inventory turns over faster, making it difficult to keep sufficient inventory in stock (stock-outs).

In addition, suppliers may not be able to keep up with increased demand. This may require the addition of new suppliers to the supply management chain. If a company increases the number of suppliers for raw material inventory, trying to manage quality from several sources becomes more cumbersome.

If there is a stock-out, how does the company handle back orders? Fast-growth companies usually experience increased levels of back orders as a result of increased volume of demand. Some components needed for a product may be in stock, whereas other components are out of stock. Unfortunately, this means that the company's working capital is tied up in unusable inventory. Inventory turnover begins to decrease for some components and thus raise the cost base. Once the needed inventory comes in, tracking it may be difficult given the increased number of back orders.

Inefficient procurement. As a company becomes more desperate to fill orders, the purchasing department may be forced to obtain raw materials any way it can. In the end, purchasing agents lose control of managing suppliers and may be willing to pay almost any price just to get their hands on sufficient raw materials to meet demand. Sometimes companies get into a situation of panic buying. They forget about quality and don't think about freight. They have a "we need it yesterday" mentality.

In addition, when a company is going through a period of rapid growth, it may hedge too aggressively because managers are afraid of running out of inventory. Rather than using effective inventory management techniques, managers may carry too much inventory. The result is that the cost of capital associated with carrying unnecessary inventory raises the cost base.

Many companies try to combat inventory management problems by trying to implement a new inventory control system during times of fast growth. Implementing new systems as a reaction to growing pains (as opposed to planning the implementation of a new system in advance) is usually a surefire way to fail. When a purchasing department is under extreme pressure to fill the shelves with inventory, employees will abandon newer technologies and revert back to old habits because that's what they know best. It is much more effective to implement a new inventory control system when extreme pressure subsides.

Poor customer relations. When demand increases rapidly, salespeople stop being salespeople and start acting as order takers. They become overworked and uninspired.

Salespeople are a company's link to the outside world. Often salespeople are the only company representatives that customers see. Major problems can arise in a fast-growth company when salespeople don't have the right environment to do their job effectively. This problem escalates when salespeople don't share the same success as the company—when their compensation is not linked to results. They end up working harder for the same pay.

The personal relationships that salespeople have built with customers over the years begin to erode. An impersonal environment replaces friendships. Moreover, when more orders come in than expected, customer service representatives scramble to fill orders. Employees that were once polite and friendly to customers are now short and abrupt. They finish with one customer as quickly as possible so they can get to the next customer who has patiently been waiting on hold for 10 minutes.

Staffing needs. As a company grows, so do demands on existing and new employees. Employees may feel overworked. Realistically, if the company doesn't plan effectively for managing growth, an employee may end up doing the work of two.

Skills change, too. Certain skills were needed to grow the business but often a different set of skills is required to manage growth. Managers that helped grow the company may not be able to make the transition—they may become obsolete.

Workloads become unbalanced. Everyone is stressed and human resources managers are desperately trying to keep several balls in the air at once. Overtime starts to become the norm. This can often become extremely excessive and the cost base begins to rise because the company is paying significant resources for overtime.

Another problem with staffing during periods of fast growth is training new employees. Often in a fast-growth environment, new employees suffer baptism by fire—they learn as they go. This opens up a company to numerous mistakes and inconsistencies. Recall the earlier example of Floyd Feezell, Steve Chamberlain, and Perry Shea, who were working for an engineering company that grew at an average rate of over 50 percent for six years in a row. Numerous problems associated with fast growth started eroding the company. Rapid growth necessitated bringing in new employees and putting them on the front line before they were ready. The company lost all sense of continuity and ultimately customers became frustrated. Growth eventually took its toll. As Feezell recalls, "Internal stresses developed [from fast growth] and the company essentially split in half." Eventually Feezell, Chamberlain, and Shea had to spin off a new company.

Integration Issues: Communication Breakdowns and Problems in Decision Making

One of the most common, and most critical, growing pains a company will encounter when experiencing fast growth is difficulty with integration. This may result in poor internal communication and/or poor decision making at all levels. When everyone is so involved in playing catch-up, no one has time to make decisions. Eventually, the company becomes less and less integrated. Managers are off doing their own thing and the left hand doesn't know what the right hand is doing.

Everyone is so involved in day-to-day activities—or even trying to catch up with yesterday's activities—that the ship is running without a captain. Even if the top management team had the time to step back and make corporate-level decisions, odds are that when a company is growing out of control, the team doesn't have the information it needs to make decisions. So what happens when managers don't have the information to make decisions? They start stalling, they drag their feet. Decisions aren't made. This is dangerous to any company but could be fatal to a company experiencing fast growth.

Lack of integration and communication breakdowns during fast growth basically stem from three related factors—infrastructural problems, overburdened information technology systems, and poor financial reporting, as shown earlier in Figure 8.2.

Infrastructural problems. Organizational infrastructure can apply to many different areas. In terms of warning signs for bad growth, infrastructure issues relate to organizational structure, inappropriate empowerment, dilution of culture, and, finally, interdepartmental communication.

When many companies grow, their organizational structures subtly become flatter and flatter. The CEO adds new managers to the management team; rather than 5 people reporting to the CEO, now it's 10 or perhaps 15. The CEO's span of control increases exponentially. Everyone reports to the leader, and eventually the leader loses control. Because all decisions go through the CEO, the CEO ultimately becomes a roadblock to progress. I was once working with a billion-dollar company whose CEO was still approving any expenditure over $200.

In addition to problems for the CEO, growth that happens too fast can create another structural problem: inappropriate empowerment. In a fast-growth setting, one department may fail at completing a key task, so the task is delegated to someone who can get the job done quickly. Sometimes, this type of delegation can be appropriate but other times not; however, in the long run, as this type of activity continues, delegation eventually starts to become disconnected from appropriate departments. Good workers, regardless of their area of expertise, are put under the gun because they are the ones who can get the job done. Good workers start to wear too many hats, but they are still given more tasks because speed is of the essence—growth is happening too fast. Errors start to occur, quality starts to slip. Unfortunately, what happens some of the time is that companies become so dependent on certain individuals that these individuals become overworked and overstressed—and eventually burn out.

Yet another structural concern during periods of fast growth is the potential dilution of a company's organizational culture. The environment that drove a company to success in the first place slowly vanishes. Flexibility and risk taking can be discouraged during times of fast growth. Procedures become formalized to try to gain back control. New employees are hired, many of them in administrative roles, and more layers are added to the company. Before they know it, managers have lost the culture they worked so hard to create. Moreover, what was once a flexible, adaptable structure has, out of necessity, become a rigid bureaucracy of many layers.

Finally, as structures evolve to meet growing demand, communication both within and between departments suffers. Ultimately, no one knows what's going on in other parts of the company. What was once a well-oiled, integrated machine is now a company in chaos. Do salespeople know what types of promotions the marketing department is running? Is the marketing department aware of margins so they know if the company is making a profit on the items that are being advertised? Do the operations and logistics departments understand the promises that salespeople are making? Does the purchasing department know the strains that the operations department must overcome to meet demand? The bottom line is that when a company experiences fast growth, integration becomes a key issue.

Does that mean that a fast-growth company needs to design the perfect structure before it pursues fast growth? The answer, surprisingly, is no. One of the biggest traps for companies about to embark on fast growth is to be overly optimistic. They invest in highly complex systems and overextend themselves. Growth doesn't materialize as projected and the companies come crashing down. In contrast, growth champions remain flexible. They proactively build new systems, but these systems evolve as the company evolves rather than achieving 100 percent closure on everything before the company moves forward.

Overburdened information technology systems. As a company experiences fast growth, everyone looks to the information technology department for help. The hope is that somehow, someway, information technology experts will come to the rescue, somehow creating miracles to get the company back on track. Seldom does this happen. Why? Because the information technology department becomes overwhelmed—many times disproportionately more than most other areas in a company.

The information technology people are overworked and what used to take days to do may now take weeks or even months. So in order to keep their heads above water, managers from everywhere in the company do whatever they can to try to keep afloat. Because the information technology group is so overburdened, combined with the stresses of fast growth, managers are forced to put together their own stand-alone systems to keep the ball rolling. Instead of being integrated with the rest of the company, managers are forced to do their own thing and thus disconnect themselves from the rest of the company. Two employees may be sitting five feet away from each other, but neither knows what the other is doing; and often they end up doing the same job. Repetition becomes the norm and inefficiencies skyrocket. Recall that in Chapter 4 I talked about redundancy as a technique intentionally pursued by growth companies trying to increase creativity and flexibility. This is quite different than unintentionally doing the same activity twice. The key difference is redundancy, for flexibility and creativity are long-term oriented (letting people dream dreams), whereas unintentional repetition from inefficiency is usually short-term oriented—redundancy in day-to-day tasks.

Meanwhile, at the top of the hierarchy the management team is now clueless. Systems running independently of the company network go unreported. With numerous departments doing their own thing, the result is poor (if any) information filtering to upper-level management. Making sound decisions becomes virtually impossible at a time when making sound decisions is critical to the future survival of the company.

If a company tries to keep control and is somehow able to integrate new computers into the companywide network during times of fast growth, the system may get stretched so far that it crashes—frequently. When the system is down, the company is down. And routine procedures, such as backing up system information at the end of the day, are abandoned because employees are too busy taking care of frontline demands. Another problem with information technology when a company experiences fast growth is that the system falls behind the times. New versions of software are coming out at lightning speed. It can be embarrassing when a customer's software is several versions more advanced than yours, and you find out your system can't communicate with their system anymore.

Poor financial reporting. Many times during periods of fast growth, because everyone is so busy trying to keep up with expansion, internal financial controls are compromised. A red flag for any company experiencing fast growth is when the finance department starts to provide management with high volumes of raw data rather than interpreted information that management can use in decision making. Like many other departments, finance and accounting feel tremendous pressures with increasing demand. Forecasts have to be recalculated, budgets have to be reconsidered, cash flow projections need to be refigured, and statements need to be reconciled.

What was once a routine job has suddenly become a cluttered mess. In the past, the finance department transformed raw data into usable information (e.g., tables and graphs). Accountants also provided interpretations of the information so management could use it for decision making. However, as a company experiences fast growth, the effectiveness of the finance function diminishes.

Some people may think, "So what, finance is not a line function anyway," or "We can ramp up finance after we get a grip on operations and marketing." Don't managers need to have financial information in order to make decisions about where to ramp up operations? It seems as though a period when accurate financial information becomes most critical is the exact time when many companies abandon it.

Once a company loses control of its financial management, it loses control of cost management. As we have discussed in previous chapters, costs can quickly increase at exponential rates as a company experiences fast growth. Letting go of financial management is the first step in letting this happen.

To understand the problem, many companies rely on a scorecard approach to fiscally manage their companies in times of rapid growth.[5] A simple scorecard approach can be composed of a few sets of measures to make sure the company is financially sound. Specific metrics commonly used can be seen in Figure 8.3. A scorecard approach integrates management and accounting so that management can make effective decisions to guide the growth of the company.

What do well-managed companies do once they have the scorecard measures? They develop a process to *routinely* com-

FIGURE 8.3 Financial Scorecard Approach to Measure Financial Health

Type of Measure	Rationale	Metrics
Operations Measures	Used to understand productivity issues	Sales per employee Asset turnover Inventory turnover Production output Cost of goods sold
Performance Measures	Used to understand performance and resource allocation issues	Return on assets Return on investment Return on sales Return on equity
Liquidity Measures	Used to measure ability to meet short-term cash obligations	Current ratio Quick ratio
Leverage Measures	Used to assess the ability to effectively manage debt and borrow additional capital	Debt/equity Debt/assets Time interest earned
Market Value Measures	Used to measure performance impact on shareholder value	Price/earnings Market-to-book price

pare these measures against previously established benchmarks. They create decision-making processes for using information from the scorecard to make any changes to strategies.

One word of caution: When using benchmarks, don't fall into the generic benchmark trap; generic benchmark measures are typically found in popular accounting articles and books. According to these sources, it is widely understood that a current ratio (used to measure liquidity as seen in Figure 8.3) greater than a score of 2 is satisfactory and a score below 2 is unsatisfactory. This information is too generic. A company like Boeing has a current ratio (current assets/current liabilities) of 1.15. Using the generic benchmark of 2, management should feel that the company needs to improve its liquidity position; however, when you consider that Boeing is in a very capital-intensive industry and has assets in excess of $36 billion, a liquidity ratio of less than 2 doesn't seem too bad.

Conversely, a company like Microsoft is in software development and therefore capital intensity for it is not as great as for an airplane manufacturer. Consequently, its liquidity ratio is 2.32. Last year the liquidity ratio was about 3. Is that too high? No, in less capital-intensive businesses, financial measures will change.

In addition, when using the financial measures in Figure 8.3 to understand warning signs associated with fast growth, another key consideration for a growth company is effective cash flow management. Despite the importance of analyzing income statements and balance sheets, survival of a growing business may be highly dependent on cash flows rather than net income. Other considerations for managers to keep them in the loop include:

- Actual budgets versus forecasts and budgets

- Sales statistics

- Staffing needs

- Credit limits

- Purchase trends

- Product availability

Impact of Growth on Financial Measures: Being a Realist

Growth costs money. In the short run, every one of the measures I just discussed may be depressed by growth. Companies often invest significant resources in order to grow. This investment hurts cash flow, which in turn hurts liquidity ratios. If the business has to borrow money to grow, leverage measures will be hurt. And in the short run, performance measures may drop given the significant amount of capital necessary to grow. Bottom line: In the short run, growth may need to be fueled by cash; therefore, management needs to be realistic in terms of short-term financial expectations.

Do you still want to grow? Don't let the downsides of growth discourage your desire. Most of the downsides discussed in this chapter can be virtually eliminated through a well-balanced business plan presented in the next chapter. As we have discussed numerous times already, in the long run, growth can provide significant benefits, but before you blindly pursue a new growth opportunity, ask yourself—*really* ask yourself—"Are we ready to grow right now?"

Endnotes

1. Laurie A. Shuster, "Growing Pains," *Civil Engineering* (May 1999): 64–65.

2. "Plant Floor Success," *Industry Week* 24, no. 11, 40.

3. Ibid.

4. Ibid.

5. Chris Malburg, "Surviving Explosive Growth," *Journal of Accountancy* (December 1997): 67–72.

Walking the Tightrope

A Balanced Game Plan for Sustainable Growth

By now I hope you have realized that there is no secret for attaining and sustaining growth. It's not simply a manager's ability to see opportunities or externally frame markets. It goes beyond creating a growth attitude and having great leadership. It is more than competing to get a bigger piece of the pie and innovating value to make the pie bigger.

Although each of these components is critical to growth, they are just that—components. Each set of growth catalysts— markets, organizational capabilities, and strategies—are important pieces of the puzzle. One without the others will only lead to short-term growth.

> **G**rowth without balance may be worse than no growth at all.

The three sets of growth catalysts interact with each other and build off of each other to simultaneously propel fast growth. It is the ability of companies to manage these catalysts—all of them—that leads to fast, sustainable growth. Throughout this book, I've talked about the importance of balance. If one concept comes the closest to being the secret to sustainable growth, it is *balance*. The ability to balance markets, organization capabilities, and strategies is the one common factor that generates sustainable, value-driven growth. Trying to pursue one aspect of growth rather than focusing on balance among all three catalysts is like losing your brakes as you're driving down a steep mountain. You become dependent on your environment, desperately reacting to each turn in the road. Somehow you can manage to stay on the road for a while, but as you pick up speed, sooner or later you lose control and come to a crashing halt.

Balance: The Difference between Attaining Growth and Sustaining Growth

Don't you think it seems ironic that growth champions don't focus on growth? Many companies that strive for success focus exclusively on growth, and then, to their dismay, they get what they wished for. As noted in the last chapter, growth for the sake of growth will hurt most companies more than it will help them. In contrast, *growth champions focus on balance, not growth*. I've talked about balance throughout this book. Every chapter has identified factors that need to be in balance for a business to sustain growth (e.g., balance between incremental and leap-growth strategies, balance between growth opportunities and operations, and balance between internal growth and external growth).

I've talked about numerous ways to attain growth as well as numerous ways to sustain growth. The multitude of balanc-

---

FIGURE 9.1   The Ten Balancing Acts to Sustainable Growth

Balancing to Attain Growth
- Balance between customers and competition
- Balance between looking outside-in and looking inside-out
- Balance between incremental growth and leap growth
- Balance between internal growth and external growth

Balancing to Sustain Growth
- Balance between growth and operations
- Balance between growth and cost management
- Balance between top-line growth and bottom-line profits
- Balance between flexibility and control
- Balance between opportunism and realism

Balancing between Attaining and Sustaining Growth
- Balancing among markets, capabilities, and strategies

---

ing acts that a growth champion has to juggle to stay ahead of the pack can be broken down into three categories:

1. Balance that leads to attaining growth

2. Balance that leads to sustaining growth

3. Balance between attaining growth and sustaining growth

A summary of different balance considerations can be seen in Figure 9.1.

How can a company expect to simultaneously manage all of these different balancing acts? Specifically, how do growth champions achieve balance across such diverse areas? How do they achieve maximum balance and sustain growth and profitability in the long term?

Numerous factors can influence business growth. Therefore, it's no surprise that occasionally we become overwhelmed by the complexities associated with trying to grow a business. Surprisingly little has been said about balance as a critical consideration in the effective pursuit of growth. Sustainable growth starts with a fundamental understanding of the different aspects of balance and finishes with a pragmatic, step-by-step process that provides a blueprint for success. It is the accumulation of these steps that leads to greatness. Therefore, the remainder of this chapter will focus on the ten key aspects of balance and a systematic approach (listed in Figure 9.1) to put this knowledge into a winning action plan.

Balance as a Means to Attain Growth

Before a business needs to concern itself with controlling growth, it has to figure out a way to attain growth. I've talked about different ways to view markets as well as numerous places to look for growth opportunities. Four central balancing issues pertain to the pursuit of growth opportunities: balance between customers and competition, using an outside-in versus inside-out perspective, incremental growth and leap growth, and internal growth versus external growth.

Balance between Customers and Competition

There is nothing wrong with attempting to develop advantages over competitors to attain incremental growth. Many average businesses do just that. They try to develop advantages by focusing on what competitors do. Realistically, however, this type of activity rarely leads to leap growth.

Growth champions achieve a unique balance between focusing on customers versus focusing on competitors. Admittedly, they know where their competitors are at any given time, but their primary focus is on innovating value for customers.

Competition is just one of many factors they use to understand their markets; however, customers are the most important. Focusing on value rather than competitors puts customers on center stage.

By focusing on customers, growth champions are able to develop radically new ways to define value. Also, by focusing on innovating value, growth champions consider the needs of current customers *and* noncustomers. Companies focusing on competition rarely consider noncustomers. Rather, they are too worried about losing current customers, resulting in an "if it isn't broke, don't fix it" mentality.

To deliver value rather than benchmarking competitors and then trying to do better, growth champions develop value far beyond incremental improvements. In terms of balance between customers and competitors, they put much more emphasis on the customer side, although being a value innovator doesn't mean you should completely ignore competitors. It would not be wise to ignore competition, but competition should be kept in the periphery rather than becoming a focal point. As seen in Figure 9.2, for a growth champion, balance between customers and competitors is actually a state of disequilibrium where customers come first. Growth champions believe that if you take care of the customer, competition should take care of itself.

Sometimes, serving the customer means that you have to think of competition in nontraditional ways. Many executives interpret the traditional view of strategy by perceiving competition as the enemy. If competition makes a move, they retaliate via imitation. Their organizations become chameleons, simply reacting to their environment rather than focusing on increasing customer value.

Instead of viewing competition as the enemy, many growth companies are now finding numerous opportunities to create value by *cooperating* with competitors. The auto industry has been doing this for years (e.g., Toyota and General Motors; Daim-

FIGURE 9.2   Value Innovation through Disequilibrium

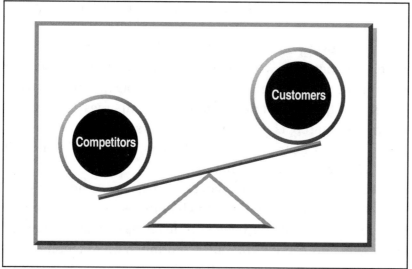

ler and Chrysler; and, recently, General Motors, Ford Motor Company, and Chrysler).

This sums it up pretty well by using an analogy with the game Rock, Scissors, Paper. Sometimes it's OK to knock heads with competitors, but growth champions know that it's also OK to extend a hand if it's necessary to successfully innovate value for customers. Instead of foregoing an opportunity just because you have to let a competitor in on the deal, isn't it better that you both win?

Competition	Cooperation
Paper smothers stone	Paper cradles stone
Stone smashes scissors	Stone sharpens scissors
Scissors slash paper.	Scissors transform paper

Balance between Looking Outside-In and Looking Inside-Out

In the past, looking outside-in was considered forward thinking. Now it's the norm. Growth champions achieve success by balancing an effective outside-in perspective with a leading-edge inside-out perspective. In contrast to most average companies, it's much more than simply taking an outside-in view of the world. Growth-oriented companies are able to look at themselves from an outside-in perspective, much as a customer would view them, but they balance their outside-in perspective with an inside-out perspective that gives them the ability to know their business better than anyone else does. They supercharge their outside-in knowledge with appropriate inside-out knowledge—namely, an unparalleled level of expertise. Balance between an outside-in perspective and an inside-out perspective allows growth champions to anticipate customers' needs.

Balance between Incremental Growth and Leap Growth

Successful growth companies must achieve balance between incremental growth and leap growth. Incremental growth often produces the resources and stability necessary for pursuing leap growth. Rather than focusing on competition to get a bigger piece of the pie, leap-growth strategies focus on ways to make the pie bigger, allowing significant long-term growth opportunities. Growth champions manage to achieve an extraordinary balance between these two types of strategies. Incremental-growth strategies provide them stability and the capital to fuel the fire, while leap-growth strategies provide sufficient future growth opportunities. Pursuing one type of strategy without the other simply won't cut it. You need balanced pursuit of both types of strategies to achieve sustainable growth.

Leon Dreimann, CEO of Salton, has perfected the art of balancing incremental growth and leap-growth strategies. Salton is king of the infomercial; it owns Juiceman, Toastmaster, Breadman—and how can we forget George Foreman's Lean Mean Fat-Reducing Grilling Machine? Dreimann has grown this company an average of 61 percent over the last five years, placing Salton at number three on *Business Week*'s 1999 list of hot growth companies. He is aware that some of his products provide consistent incremental cash flow, but he also realizes that to sustain growth, Salton needs a steady balance between incremental growth and leap growth.

Dreimann realizes that in the infomercial business, products come and go quickly, and therefore he is very proactive in new product development. Personally, Dreimann considers, on average, 50 new ideas a week. He admits, "We don't say no to anybody." Linda Greenblatt, managing partner at Saddlerock Partners, a New York–based hedge fund that owns a considerable number of Salton shares, says, "Dreimann gives me confidence the company [Salton] isn't a one-hit wonder." Dreimann fills his leap-growth pipeline with numerous opportunities through extraordinary balance between incremental growth and leap growth.

Another company that has achieved a solid balance between incremental growth and leap growth is Hewlett-Packard. The result is that over the last five years, H-P has averaged 13.4 percent growth in sales and 11 percent growth in profits. In terms of balance, H-P's growth has been generated by a strong commitment to research and development in electronics and computer technology. H-P capitalizes on balance by providing a rapid flow of new products and services to markets it already serves and by expanding into new areas that build on existing technologies, competencies, and customer interests. In addition, H-P actively pursues emerging opportunities in related fields.

Balance between Internal Growth and External Growth

Growth champions realize that different situations dictate different growth strategies. They don't commit to a particular strategic choice. Sometimes it makes sense to grow a new business internally. Other times, it makes more strategic sense to consider a joint venture or the acquisition of another company. The situation determines the best strategy. Therefore, growth champions achieve good balance between internal-growth strategies and external-growth strategies based on what a specific growth opportunity allows.

Earlier I mentioned that Nestlé has achieved 70 percent of its growth by entering mature markets through acquisitions in the 1990s. These acquisitions resulted in new proprietary expertise and synergies in product development and distribution channels. Consequently, Nestlé plans to achieve 70 percent of its growth over the next decade through internal development strategies. Nestlé is letting the situation dictate the best relationship strategy, which is typical of most growth champions.

Balance as a Means to Sustain Growth

I've talked about good growth and bad growth. Good growth is controlled growth that leads to bottom-line profitability. Bad growth is uncontrolled and can actually destroy a company that is not prepared to handle its high demands. Five central balancing issues pertain to a company's ability to manage and sustain controlled growth: balance between growth and operations; growth and cost management; top-line growth and bottom-line profits, flexibility and control, and opportunism and realism.

Balance between Growth and Operations

It is not enough to achieve growth. Growth champions are able to simultaneously pursue (1) growth goals to increase revenues and (2) operations goals to manage growth. If operations aren't ramped up to manage new growth, a company's cost base may increase, delivery times may suffer, quality will usually slip, and eventually growth can become a manager's worst nightmare.

Growth champions are very good at making sure that operations are continuously improved to meet the demands of growth, which means that at times they are willing to give up a growth opportunity. Howard Schultz, chairman and CEO of Starbucks, could grow his business much faster than its typical 50 percent annual rate if he wanted to through franchising. Schultz has decided that Starbucks won't franchise, use artificially flavored coffees, or partner with the hundreds of businesses that bang on its doors every week. You'd be surprised at the variety of companies that try to jump on Starbucks' bandwagon. Schultz explains, "Over the short term these steps would drive up revenues and profits. But over the long term, they would be a giant mistake." According to Ronald Henkoff of *Fortune* magazine, Schultz is concerned that if his company grows too fast, he will lose control over quality of the coffees and management of the brand name, which could hurt the company's reputation.

Because of its explosive growth, Amazon has faced numerous issues of finding the correct balance between operations and growth. Vice President of Information Technology Charlie Bell at Amazon says, "The hardest nut to crack is meeting demands of customers and scaling [operations]. You don't want to strangle the business with the process."

How can companies overcome this challenge? Richard Schwartz, chief technology officer of Vignette, a large vendor of Web servers, says, "Invest enough up front so you can keep growing." Growth champions ramp up operations as vigorously as they pursue sales growth. They know that one without the other is like playing with fire—sooner or later, you'll get burned.

Balance between Growth and Cost Management

Growth champions realize that growth and cost management are not mutually exclusive. A cost-cutting mentality can be devastating to growth, but losing track of cost management can be devastating to the survival of a company. Consider the experience of Benjamin Cohen, the founder of Logic Works, a company whose record growth wasn't good news. Logic Works didn't maintain a balance between growth and operations; and when a company becomes unbalanced, bad things are bound to happen.

In early 1995, things were going great. Cohen's software company was growing at warp speed; he appeared on the cover of *Business Week* because Logic Works was named one of the top growth companies that year. In just four years he had built his software business into a $40 million superstar. The firm literally skyrocketed with revenues, growing at a rate of over 100 percent per year. By 1995, revenues were at $30.7 million, up 131 percent from 1994. Demand for Cohen's database program, ERWin, was huge; his salespeople spent all of their time taking orders. It was a classic example of a pull market—no solicitation was necessary—and demand just seemed to happen.

While this all sounds wonderful, Cohen's company was just riding a wave. Arguably, he had a good product—no, make that a *great* product—and there was huge demand. The company grew like crazy. Unfortunately, Logic Works didn't understand the importance of balance between growth and operations.

In 1996, sales started off with a bang—$12 million in the first quarter. In the second quarter of 1996, sales began to lag. And Logic Works wasn't paying attention to operations, so costs began to soar. Operating expenses nearly doubled. And the company didn't have strategies in place to effectively do what it had previously accomplished—exploit growth opportunities.

All of a sudden, the company found itself in a new role. Rather than aggressively focusing on fast growth, the company found itself reactively focusing on operations. In the second half of 1996, the company was forced to focus on restructuring and severe cost-cutting measures. Eventually, the inability to balance growth and operations cost Cohen his job.

Ultimately, Logic Works understood the importance of balance. Unfortunately, it learned the hard way. With its costs back in line, the company again successfully realigned itself for growth. New management pursued controlled growth rather than reacting to unanticipated growth. Gregory Peers, serving as the interim CEO after Cohen's departure, stated that the skills needed to create a small high-tech company are not the same as the skills necessary to manage an industry giant.

In 1998, Logic Works again had the industry's best-selling data modeling solution with ERWin. This time, however, the company had a good balance between growth and operations. The company became a big winner that year when it was acquired by PLATINUM Technology. A year later, management won again when PLATINUM was acquired by Computer Associates International.

Balance between Top-Line Growth and Bottom-Line Profits

As noted in the last chapter, companies that pursue growth for the sake of growth will end up losers. Growth champions pursue growth for the sake of increasing value, but even growth champions may have to develop the skill of driving profit from growth over time. Starbucks' president, Orin Smith, states, "We're going to have to look at more opportunities to grow earnings, how to manage the bottom line, not the top line. We're looking for efficiencies in manufacturing and distribution. We're reengineering."[1] Starbucks, one of the most successful growth champions mentioned in this book, is making a concerted effort to drive value rather than growth. Is it surprising that Starbucks is focusing on profitability in addition to growth? Absolutely not. Companies that become growth champions realize that balance between top-line growth and bottom-line profit must go hand in hand in order to succeed.

Balance between Flexibility and Control

Many firms strive for flexibility because flexible organizational structures encourage creativity. Other firms strive for increased control because control leads to effective cost management. Unfortunately, the more flexible an organization tries to be, the less control it has, resulting in poor cost management. Conversely, as a company becomes more control oriented, it loses flexibility. Many growth champions enjoy the best of both worlds. Flexibility and control are by no means mutually exclusive and growth champions have figured out ways to balance them.

Netscape provides an example of a growth champion that has learned, through trial and error, how to effectively achieve a balance between the flexibility of a small start-up and the control of a multibillion-dollar company. Its approach has been to continually decentralize, breaking its organizational structure into many small teams. Netscape's intent in committing to a team approach is to have large-company cost-control systems while still maintaining flexibility and creativity through the creation of numerous small teams.

As the company began to grow in size, product divisions replaced functional groups. Flexibility was critical to Netscape as the Internet evolved. Speed was paramount as the company tried to stay at the leading edge of Internet technology. Teaming provided the only legitimate platform to keep the flexibility needed for speed while maintaining the ability to coordinate and control a big business. Rather than functional-level constraints found in most organizations, small autonomous teams allow Netscape to focus on a common business.

Giving a sufficient amount of freedom to the team is critical. Empowerment increases a feeling of ownership. The more employees take ownership, the more pride they take in completing their tasks. Also, critical to Netscape's ability to balance flexibility and control has been its uncanny timing. When Netscape reached astronomical growth rates, the company was spinning out of control. Still, Jim Barksdale, Netscape's CEO, realized that moving too quickly toward a highly centralized and controlled environment could discourage creativity. "[At Netscape] moving in this direction was a delicate balancing act." Barksdale recalls:

> The trick is to know when do you bring on the bureaucrats. There's a stage in a company's life where it's fine to be loosely controlled. There's another stage where you have to get more and more serious. What you don't want to do is get too serious too soon. That stifles a lot of things.[2]

In addition to the teaming approach used by Netscape, Hewlett-Packard is very serious about communications as an effective tool to balance flexibility and control. Communications is at the core of its culture. Management believes that given the right tools, training, and information to do a good job, people will contribute their best. H-P has shown that open communication leads to strong teamwork.

> *W*hile it may be difficult to achieve good balance between flexibility and control, growth champions are able to figure out ways to have the best of both worlds.

FIGURE 9.3   Process for Balancing Flexibility and Control

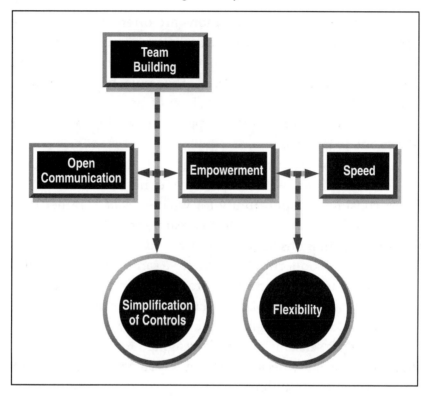

Most of the time, having the best of both worlds is not based on leading-edge technological advancements reserved for the most brilliant companies. Instead, growth champions often go back to the basics. As I've discussed, growth champions know the importance of open communication. Open communication leads to better team building and simplification of formal controls. I've also noted that growth champions are excellent at pushing down leadership in an organization (empowerment) to create growth domains. This in turn leads to improvements in speed and gives employees a sense of pride and ownership. The flow diagram in Figure 9.3 illustrates the progression many growth champions go through to achieve a proper balance between flexibility and control.

Balance between Opportunism and Realism

Leaders of growth champions are often able to balance their desire to be opportunists with the conservatism of realists. They must try to identify growth opportunities that others don't see—they must be entrepreneurial. They must be able to anticipate needs and innovate value. Part of being opportunistic means that leaders of growth companies are willing to stick their necks out, to take risks.

Leaders of growth champions are able to balance this urge to be opportunistic with the levelheadedness of realists. They must consider an opportunity for what it *could be* rather than what they *wish it* to be. It's OK to dream—and effective leaders of growth champions have the ability to identify great entrepreneurial growth opportunities. But these same leaders must also determine if these opportunities are feasible and have the possibility to increase profitability and ultimately shareholder value. In addition, they must ensure that new growth opportunities make *strategic* sense. It is very shortsighted to pursue a growth opportunity simply because you think you could make a quick buck. Trying to be all things to all people is dangerous. Growth champions choose their opportunities wisely.

Balance between Attaining and Sustaining Growth: Managing the Catalysts

Realistically, if a business wants to become a growth champion, it can't separate the balance needed to attain growth from the balance needed to sustain growth. Nor can it separate the three growth catalysts: markets, organizational capabilities, and strategies. Each catalyst has a direct impact on growth *and* each catalyst is tightly interrelated with the other catalysts. Trying to separate them will only discourage growth. Companies that don't achieve balance between the catalysts are quite often like shooting stars—an individual catalyst may drive growth for a while but eventually the opportunity will fade away and the company will too. However, figuring out a way to simultaneously manage these three catalysts can sustain long-term growth and transform an ordinary company into an extraordinary company.

Samsung Electronics has achieved extraordinary balance between managing market, organizational, and strategy catalysts. The company consistently invests in product development, technology development (for both products and processes), and marketing.

The company was founded as a member of the Samsung Group in 1969 and quickly integrated the three growth catalysts. The result: Since 1971, Samsung has grown at an average rate of 38 percent per year, expanding from monochrome television to other forms of consumer electronics, home appliances, computers, and semiconductors.

To achieve balance, Samsung's founder B. C. Lee identified three major initiatives:

1. Acquire the necessary market and technical expertise

2. Invest in production systems

3. Become competitive in a global market

Acquire the necessary market and technical expertise. The company was able to quickly develop strong knowledge of its markets and simultaneously develop leading-edge expertise in products, primarily through reverse engineering. Ultimately, Samsung accelerated its technical abilities from reverse engineering to advanced innovation in consumer electronics. Combining market knowledge and technical expertise created an effective external frame for Samsung. Value innovation allowed Samsung to see growth opportunities that others didn't see. *Samsung excelled in using the market catalyst.*

Invest in production systems. Lee invested a considerable amount of resources to build advanced manufacturing systems in terms of scale and scope. He acquired production expertise by learning critical manufacturing technologies that allowed Samsung to produce high-quality products while maintaining effective cost management systems. Specifically, Samsung realized economies of scale and scope by creating a vertically integrated manufacturing system structured to support the mass production of televisions. Samsung was very proactive in managing its capabilities. *Samsung excelled in using the organizational capability catalyst.*

Become competitive in a global market. Finally, Samsung segmented its markets very effectively, developing strategies to serve the needs of customers in each segment. The company combined the use of internal development strategies and joint venture strategies to initially export to foreign markets, accounting for about 60 percent of its revenue base. Samsung initially competed on price, then quality, and then technology. *Samsung excelled in using the strategy catalyst.*

Samsung Electronics simultaneously excels in all three sets of catalysts. This balance has allowed the company to sustain extraordinary growth over a very long period of time.

Stall Points

Samsung is unique because it has been able to maintain a high growth rate as it has become large. As most companies grow in size, maintaining growth becomes increasingly difficult. A recent study, "Stall Points: Barriers to Growth for Large Corporate Enterprises," performed by the Corporate Advisory Board in conjunction with Hewlett-Packard, examined the 50 largest companies in the world.[3] It concluded that almost every company occasionally encounters stall points. Stall points occur when a fast-growth company slows to a moderate growth rate.

It is rare that a company can maintain double-digit growth year in and year out. According to the study, as companies become larger, stall points last longer. The study concluded that as companies approach the $20 billion mark, double-digit growth becomes extremely difficult to maintain.

The critical importance of stall points is their impact on a company's market value. If investors are used to double-digit growth and all of a sudden the company slows to single-digit growth, the stock price will take a bigger hit than when an average company's growth rate slows. Investors have higher expectations for fast-growth companies.

When companies (of any size) hit the wall, how can they scale it? Balance between different forms of growth—namely, incremental versus leap growth and internal versus external growth. Balance helped Samsung avoid stall points and numerous other companies work through stall points.

Dream It, Do It: Creating an Action Plan for Fast Growth

It sounds so overwhelming—trying to achieve balance at so many levels. It has to be highly complex, right? But growth champions are able to pull it off. How do they do it? They do it by writing out goals and objectives and then figuring out alternative ways to achieve them. They do this *before* growth occurs. Successful growth doesn't happen because of a single event. It's the accumulation of a lot of small victories. If you walk past a construction site where a bricklayer puts down the very first brick, you may be in awe of the job ahead. But patiently and persistently, the bricklayer keeps plugging away. Eventually the building gets done and each brick is vital in carrying the load of the wall. Patiently and persistently, growth champions keep plugging away, too. The accumulation of a lot of small steps results in a winning plan to attain *and* sustain growth.

As many companies begin this process, they become impatient, wanting to reap huge rewards right away. Remember, before fast growth occurs, a company should be balanced—not perfectly balanced (that would be unrealistic) but balanced enough to control growth.

To begin the task of putting together a winning action plan for growth, there are five basic foundations I stress with my clients:

1. Keep it simple

2. Don't beat things to death

3. Prioritize

4. Set goals that initiate action

5. Make people accountable

Keep It Simple

An effective action plan should provide simplicity, not complexity. I have seen a lot of strategic plans over the years, and most of them take a fairly complex situation and make it even more complex. Companies develop expansive flow diagrams, strategic issue maps, and flow charts that are so complex they resemble a bowl of spaghetti. My head starts to hurt when I see these tools. I don't have a prayer of trying to make sense out of them, and I'm a strategic planner. If I can't make sense out of them, odds are most executives won't be able to figure them out either. So the first rule in putting together a winning action plan for growth: simplification.

Find a system that works for your employees. Remember, an action plan is a communication device. At Emerson Electric, executives who live by charts and graphs are forced to put things into a simplified format. They have to come up with two neatly drawn pyramids, rightfully known as the "twin peaks." The pyramid on the left summarizes last year's growth programs. The pyramid on the right illustrates proposals for the upcoming year. Projects include new product development, new market development, acquisitions, and so on. A committee ranks the ideas by taking into consideration market potential, capacity requirements, investment needed, and payback period. The ideas that appear to be most beneficial work their way down to the bottom of the pyramid on the right and have the best chance to receive funding. George Tamke, executive vice president of Emerson's electronic business, recalls:

> In the past, every division had the same sales growth objective. We'd pick something out of the air, like 15 percent because it was a good high number. But we didn't execute new products well. We didn't assess the risks of the new technologies and new markets, and we didn't evaluate our own track record.

There are many effective ways to put together a straightforward, workable plan. In general, a well-documented strategic plan should be able to fit on a single page. If it won't fit on one page, odds are it is probably too complex.

I think that many companies get into trouble when they try to force their plan into an off-the-shelf planning model. Every company is different, and therefore every plan should be different. I have developed a general framework that I use with many of my clients that is called the Strategy Hierarchy. This model creates a platform for businesses to create winning action plans for growth and is flexible enough to fit the individual needs of each client. A generic example can be seen in Figure 9.4. Keep in mind that this is a generic version of the Strategy Hierarchy. It is management's responsibility to customize a plan to fit the needs of its particular business for the specific context.

FIGURE 9.4 Generic Example of Strategy Hierarchy

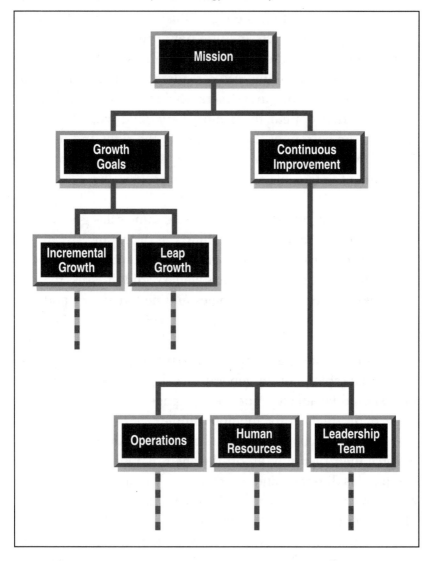

I have used various versions of this hierarchy with virtu-ally every growth company I have ever consulted with. It works well for a few reasons. First, it simplifies a complex scenario; the entire growth plan can be mapped out on one page. Second, it integrates every activity in an organization that relates to sustaining growth. Third, the process is repeatable and transfer-able. Once top management develops the company's hierarchy, lower levels of management can develop their own hierarchies that feed back into the company hierarchy. With some of my clients, we have taken the hierarchy model to extreme microlevels so that every employee in the organization can see how his or her specific job ties back into the overall strategic direction of the company.

What really makes the hierarchy so useful? It provides a means to achieve balance between every factor we have talked about in this book. For example, in Figure 9.4, note that high-level goals are separated into growth goals and continuous improvement goals. This provides excellent balance between growth and operations. On the left side of the model, growth goals are separated into incremental-growth and leap-growth strategies to again provide balance.

The generic example in Figure 9.4 presents only the first three levels in the hierarchy. Usually, when working with a client, we try to work our way down to about five levels, where each level breaks down activities from previous levels into more detail. Here are some topics to think about when moving down to lower levels in the hierarchy.

Incremental growth. Recall that incremental growth can be broken down into (1) existing and new market expansion and (2) product development strategies.

Leap growth. Leap growth can be broken down into four categories according to Figure 3.2: value innovation, diamond mining, market segmentation, and discontinuities. Each of these categories can then be broken down further (e.g., value innovation comes from developing a solid external frame, as discussed in Chapter 2. A solid external frame comes from a combination of an outside-in and inside-out perspective, and so on).

Once specific growth strategies have been selected, specific relationship strategies (Chapter 7) need to be identified to pursue growth opportunities.

Operations. Operations can incorporate a variety of diverse tasks, depending on your business. In this category of the hierarchy, many growth companies focus on creating an effective cost management program. In addition, they focus on ramping up operational efficiencies, integration, and capacity to meet the forecasted increase in demand resulting from the growth side of the hierarchy. And fiscal management and information technology should receive special attention to ensure they are ramped up to meet demand. These issues are discussed in Chapters 4 and 8.

Human resources. Human resources are probably the biggest challenge for most growth companies. According to Dianne Gresham, vice president of human resources for ATS, "The biggest challenge of a growth company is finding the people you need to grow your business." The human resources management function can be broken down into three basic activities: (1) attracting talent, (2) retaining talent, and (3) developing talent as discussed in Chapters 4 and 5.

Leadership issues. Leadership is responsible for two major areas: company infrastructure and assembling a winning top management team. Infrastructure issues can be broken down into structural concerns (e.g., maintaining balance between flexibility and control) and cultural concerns (creating a growth attitude as seen in Figure 4.1). Assembling a winning top management team revolves around designing a diverse team and playing the dual role of opportunist and realist as discussed in Chapter 5. In addition, it is the responsibility of the top management team to push leadership down to lower levels and to coordinate activities across growth domains.

The Strategy Hierarchy can be used to integrate most of the ideas from this book into a cohesive blueprint for achieving growth. Also note that sitting at the very top of the hierarchy is the company's mission. Everything, including all growth-related issues as well as all continuous improvement issues, must tie back to the company's mission. This ensures that a growth company pursues opportunities that make strategic sense rather than going off on a half-cocked adventure the company has no business being in.

Don't Beat Things to Death

It's admirable to acquire sufficient detail to measure how each strategy is progressing, but as markets change, so do good strategic plans. *Strategic planning* is actually a dangerous term because it implies a once-a-year process for many companies. Top management goes off-sight for a two-day retreat and comes back with a strategic plan. Then the plan is carefully placed on a shelf where it sits, untouched and collecting dust, until the same individuals go through the same process next year. Sound familiar?

Rather than thinking of this process as strategic planning, think of it as *strategic management,* an ongoing, fluid process. Markets are changing so fast that many managers are learning at faster rates than ever before simply to survive. As markets change and managers learn, the plan must change, too. Objectives need to be redefined as well as the tactics used to meet these objectives. In a highly dynamic industry, it may actually be dangerous to present a full-blown strategic plan to all employees because by the time the plan is distributed, it has already become obsolete.

Does that mean companies in highly dynamic industries should forget about strategic planning? Absolutely not. Strategic planning keeps companies focused on the future. What it does mean is the plan has to be fluid. While the specifics of the plan may change, usually the underlying logic (e.g., focusing on value innovation, creating a growth attitude, etc.) will not change. So in a very broad or macro sense, the plan needs to be articulated at all levels; however, at the micro level, it's the responsibility of each team to figure out how it will fit into the underlying logic of the company.

Shona Brown and Kathleen Eisenhardt, authors of *Competing on the Edge: Strategy as Structured Chaos*,[4] contend that a semi-coherent strategy results from constant change. This implies that successful plans allow for surprises, mistakes, variety, and learning along the way. They are not written in stone and the more a management team beats a plan to death, the more likely it becomes written in stone.

Prioritize

When you finally identify workable tactics at lower levels in the Strategy Hierarchy, things can become a bit overwhelming. Here you sit with 25 critical tactics, each one extremely important in terms of achieving fast, sustainable growth. So where do you go from here?

Before you can]put tactics into a workable action plan, they need to be prioritized, but prioritization can be a painful process. It is often a zero-sum situation—for one opportunity to be funded, another must be put on the back burner. An instrument that works well to prioritize objectives is a modified version of an importance/urgency matrix, a model widely used in numerous applications. For example, Stephen Covey, author of the best-seller *The 7 Habits of Highly Effective People*,[5] uses this model for personal development. A couple of years ago, when I was developing a growth plan for the Corporate Brand Equity Division at Caterpillar, a group that initially experienced growth in excess of 300 percent per year, the director, Lois Boaz, suggested using this matrix in a business application. We had identified 20 unique tactics and we were struggling to prioritize them. The matrix worked so well that since then, I use the matrix whenever prioritization becomes a roadblock. Figure 9.5 illustrates my modified version of an importance/urgency matrix.

To use the matrix effectively, I have managers identify a set of critical tactics based on lower levels in the Strategy Hierarchy and simply plot them in the matrix based on their relative short-term necessity and long-term significance to the overall success of the company. Factors in the upper right-hand quadrant (high importance and high urgency) are prioritized first in an action plan, followed by factors in the upper left-hand quadrant (high importance, low urgency).

Set Goals to Initiate Action

Don't let execution turn into talking about execution. Growth champions take action. In terms of proactively taking action, best-selling author and consultant Tom Peters explains:

> It becomes talking instead of doing. The team stops building prototypes and beta-testing and instead starts talking about what needs to happen next. Or the team spends too much time in meetings, talking to each other, and not enough time in the marketplace, talking with end users. Think of it as a math problem: If teams have a talk/do ratio of 70 percent talking and 30 percent doing, then you want to reverse those figures so that the ratio is 70 percent doing and 30 percent talking.[6]

To initiate action, each objective should have an identifiable start date, completion date, and milestones if applicable. In addition, metrics need to be established to make sure that everything is progressing as planned. As a situation changes, the metrics change, not the other way around.

FIGURE 9.5   Modified Importance/Urgency Matrix

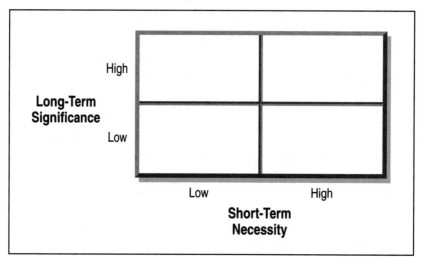

Make People Accountable

As the top management team pushes leadership down to lower levels, employees are given more responsibility. With responsibility comes authority, independence, access to information, and decision making. The more actively involved employees become in implementing a growth plan, the more accountable they have to become. You'd be surprised how serious a person becomes about meeting deadlines when an individual's name is attached to them.

An effective approach I've used to put growth plans into action and assign accountability is to think of a growth plan the same way a project manager thinks of a project. Using a Gantt Chart format as seen in Figure 9.6 is an effective way to map out specific tactics that have been previously prioritized using an importance/urgency matrix. It is also a useful tool in terms of identifying interdependencies among these tactics, timelines, and responsibilities. To ensure that specific individuals are held accountable, completion of each tactic is assigned to a single

FIGURE 9.6 Abbreviated Example of Gantt Chart Format for Growth Plan

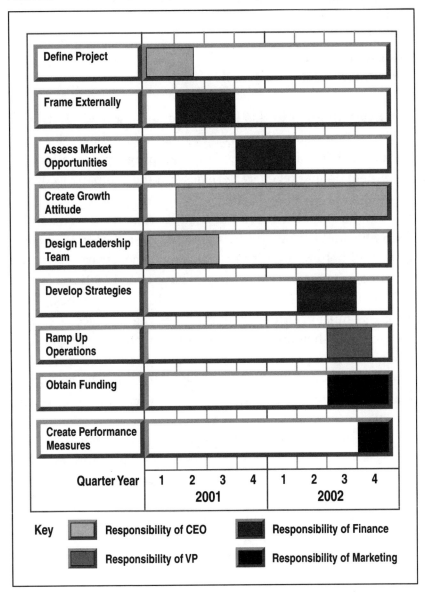

individual. Accountability can then be reinforced when the top management team meets periodically to assess the progression of the growth plan.

A Final Caveat

Every thought in this book could somehow work its way into an action plan for growth. Emphasis in a particular area, whether it is mining diamonds or ramping up operations, is dependent on market characteristics and the company's current situation.

A logical sequence should result based on the "Five Rules to Creating a Winning Plan for Growth." First, the Strategy Hierarchy will help to identify specific tactics necessary to pursue balanced growth. Once these tactics have been identified (a typical client team will average between 15 and 25 tactics), then managers must prioritize them using the significance/necessity matrix. Once they are prioritized, these tactics are put into an action plan using a Gantt Chart format to identify specific time-lines and responsibilities. At the end of the day, you should be able to walk away with a step-by-step action plan for pursuing growth.

A final reminder: the figures presented in this final section are *examples* of models that have worked successfully for companies trying to create action plans necessary to pursue growth. So rather than trying to force your company into a particular model, see how the particular model fits into your specific situation. Let common sense dictate.

Endnotes

1. Ronald Henkoff, "Growing Your Company: Five Ways to Do It Right!" *Fortune*, November 25, 1996, 78–85.

2. Ibid.

3. Corporate Advisory Board, "Stall Points: Barriers to Growth for Large Corporate Enterprises" (Washington, DC: 1998). This report was performed in conjunction with Hewlett-Packard.

4. Shona Brown and Kathleen Eisenhardt, *Competing on the Edge: Strategy as Structured Chaos.* (Boston, MA: Harvard Business School Press, 1998).

5. Stephen R. Covey, *The 7 Habits of Highly Effective People: Restoring the Character Ethic.* (New York: Simon & Schuster, 1989).

6. Tom Peters, "The Wow Project," *Fast Company* 24 (1999): 116–27.